I Cor. 10:4

W9-AXL-319

HOW TO BE HAPPY

NO MATTER WHAT

TOM WATSON, JR.

Regal Books A Division of G/L Publications
Ventura, California, U.S.A.

The foreign language publishing of all Regal books is under the direction of GLINT. GLINT provides financial and technical help for the adaptation, translation and publishing of books in more than 85 languages for millions of people worldwide.

For more information write: GLINT, P.O. Box 6688, Ventura, CA 93006.

Fifth Printing, 1981

Published by Regal Books
A Division of G/L Publications
Ventura, California 93006
Printed in U.S.A.

Library of Congress Catalog Card No. 77-73559
ISBN 0-8307-0465-5

CONTENTS

A Teacher's Manual and Student Discovery Guide for Bible study groups using this book are available from your church supplier.

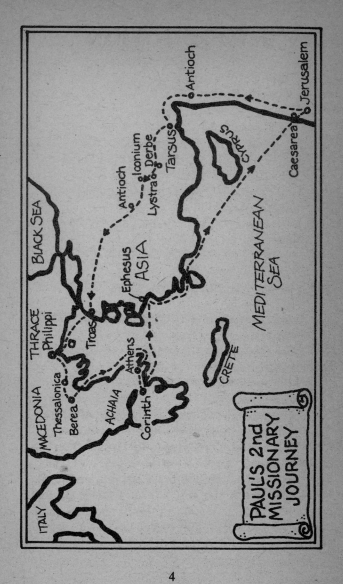

PAUL'S 2nd MISSIONARY JOURNEY

4

INTRODUCTION

If you lived in the city of Philippi in A.D. 60, you might not know very much about happiness. For one thing, you'd have to learn to speak Latin and if you flunked that your only other option would be Greek. They're what a Macedonian spoke—which is what you'd be if you lived in Philippi 1900 or so years ago.

The city was named for Philip II, father of Alexander the Great and king of Macedonia about four centuries before Paul got there with the gospel. You can find it at the north end of the Aegean Sea on a map. There were gold and silver in the foothills and fertile soil on the plains, but that wouldn't make life any more enjoyable for you unless you happened to be one of the noblemen who owned the place. You'd probably be digging the gold or plowing the fields 12 hours a day. For the average citizen of Philippi, life was a grim experience, with few comforts and no luxuries at all.

Philippi was more of a military colony than a commercial city. That is why only a few Jews lived there —which made a big difference in the way Paul and Silas went about establishing a church (see Acts 16). Paul usually found the Jewish synagogue and began by telling the Jews their Messiah had come. But there was no synagogue at Philippi, so he began by finding a place by the river where Jews were said to meet for prayer. When he got there, he found a few women, and one of these took seriously what he had to say. She was Lydia, a dealer in dyes and purple cloth.

It wasn't a very impressive beginning. However, Lydia became a believer, and she and her household were baptized. The church at Philippi was off and running. The account in Acts 16 gives the details. With convert number one, Paul and Silas got a place to stay. With convert number two (a fortune-telling slave) they ended up in jail. But that turned out okay because being in jail provided the chance to find convert number three, the Philippian jailer. He was probably the first Roman to join the church, which gave it an international flavor.

But think of the problems that could develop around people like these! What did a Jewish businesswoman, a fortune-teller (possibly a Greek slave girl) and a Roman jailer have in common? Each one would have problems enough in his own occupation, but when word got around that they were believers in Jesus Christ they were in big trouble. It wasn't really too bad to be a Jew in a Roman colony. Judaism at least was officially tolerated by the authorities. But Christianity had no acceptance at all. To the Roman authorities Jesus was a Nazarene whom they had executed as a common criminal. His followers were stubborn fanatics and troublemakers. The only good Christian was a dead Christian and the world was a better place without them!

So if life in Philippi was a drag before Paul and Silas came, it got even worse for people who believed Jesus was the Messiah. The Romans and Jews persecuted and penalized them. Their former friends—even their relatives—stopped speaking to them. Their neighbors thought them religious dingbats and either avoided them like the plague or reported them to the authorities.

So it's not surprising that when Paul wrote a letter to the Christians at Philippi he chose happiness as his theme—happiness, and how to find it even in an *un*happy situation.

It took Paul to teach them a truth like that. There was nothing theoretical about his crash course on "how-to-be-happy-no-matter-what." He lived what he taught. He proved it to be gut-level truth that really worked, even in life under pressure. He'd been there himself—in fact, he *was* there at the time he wrote the letter.

Philippians is one of Paul's prison epistles. He was either in a Roman jail or under house arrest when he dictated these words to Epaphroditus (see Phil. 2:25). He was experiencing something considerably lower than first-class citizenship himself. When he said, "I have learned the secret of being content in any and

7

every situation" (Phil. 4:12, *NIV*) he meant the bad times as well as the good times.

"There is a way to be happy," Philippians teaches us, "even when people and circumstances conspire to make us miserable." But we won't get very far into the epistle before discovering that Paul's formula for happiness depends on a very special attitude toward God. It's not just a new brand of humanistic philosophy. It's not a self-discipline that works if you're strong enough or smart enough to master the technique. The whole thing boils down to understanding what Jesus Christ is all about and learning to trust Him in the exact ways He claims He can help us.

Philippians is a happy book. It was written under the inspiration of the Holy Spirit by a very happy man. And to each one of us, it's going to be worth whatever time and energy it takes to digest these truths and make them a part of our own personal experience.

THE LOVE THAT GROWS AND SOWS

It has disappeared from anybody's list of top tens, twenties or forties, so you seldom hear it. But it was a great idea while it lasted and a right-on diagnosis of our society—what the world needs now is love, sweet love.

Most human ills will respond right away to a big dose of love, sweet love. Where love is found, happiness is not far away.

The problem is, there is not enough love to go around. There never has been. It's not that love is out of style or that people these days are too busy or too selfish to love. The reason there is so little love on the human scene is that people don't naturally have much of it to offer—not now, not in "the good old days," nor way back when Paul planted the gospel in

9

Macedonia. And that lack of love is why we experience so little happiness.

The Bible is concerned about that lack of love. God wants people to be happy. He knows love really is what makes things go better—not Coke. He *wants* things to go better for us because He loves us.

To even begin understanding love you have to consider what it means that God loves people like us. He is concerned enough about people loving each other to give love a prominent place throughout the Bible. He says we could do away with the Ten Commandments and all the other rules and regulations about how to treat others if people would only love each other (see Rom. 13:8-10).

People need that "love, sweet love," and need it badly. But we don't get much of it, and what's worse, we don't *give* much of it either. That's worse because *giving* love produces more happiness than *getting* it. The book of Philippians recognizes this fact of life right from the start.

But once we face up to the lack of love among humans we have another problem to wrestle with. That's the problem of how to get and give it. Love cannot be worked up like a sweat or an appetite. Just realizing we do not have it doesn't get it for us. So the question, "How do I learn to love?" becomes a mind-boggling proposition.

Paul has some practical suggestions.

A Word About the Author

Before he gets to the suggestions, Paul wants to identify himself and dispose of the who? what? why? questions. The letter is for all believers in Philippi, which includes the church officers as well as the ordinary folk. It is from the apostle himself.

There is no need for a formal introduction. In his letters to Christians in Rome and the region of Galatia and elsewhere, Paul states his qualifications and makes sure his readers understand his authority for writing. But that wasn't necessary for believers in Philippi. They had known him intimately and from the beginning had enjoyed an informal and loving relationship with their teacher. They knew Paul's awesome intellect and respected his disciplined commitment to Christ.

They also knew Timothy. It appears from the record in Acts 16 that Timothy traveled with Paul and Silas on their first trip to Philippi. He was recruited in the city of Lystra (Acts 16:1) and still was with them when they reached Thessalonica (Acts 17:13, 14). Timothy was often Paul's traveling companion, a zealous disciple and a loyal friend. The Philippian believers, aware of those facts, would have experienced an extra surge of interest when they read:

> *Paul and Timothy, servants of Christ Jesus,*
> *To all the saints in Christ Jesus at Philippi,*
> *together with the overseers and deacons:*
> *Grace and peace to you from God our Father*
> *and the Lord Jesus Christ* (Phil. 1:1, *NIV*).

The Power of Grace and Peace

Grace and peace? These are words that run a peculiar risk in the mouth, ears or eyes of ordinary humans. Try saying them out loud—"grace and peace." There's a comfortable quality in the combination—maybe too comfortable. The words look good on pa-

11

per, sound good when spoken, feel good when they slide across the tongue. But "grace and peace" can do all that and mean nothing in our personal experience. Words without meaning are dangerous—even deadly —and especially so when they are religious words. That's why these are risky.

The way Paul uses grace and peace in this letter brings us right down to where we live and how we feel about our experiences. Grace is God's acceptance of and goodness toward people who couldn't possibly deserve it. In fact, God's grace is the opposite of what we deserve. We deserve judgment—God gives us love and mercy.

Peace follows grace. When we receive God's grace, we experience His peace. It is an inner wholeness and health; a calm, settled feeling, a resting in our relationship with God. Fears, guilt, doubts are all swept away by God's peace.

Real happiness begins with receiving God's grace and experiencing His peace. Real love begins here too. When you experience God's love in His grace and peace, you can share that love with others. If you pour water into a glass until it is full and then keep pouring, the water will overflow and run out. That's what God's love does when we open ourselves to it.

Love's Perspective

Paul's next statement must have made every Philippian Christian think about his own feelings toward the apostle. It is a frank and honest expression of gratitude. In a way, Paul is saying "I love you." And "I love you" is one of the most disarming statements in the entire English vocabulary.

I thank my God every time I remember you. In all my prayers for all of you, I always pray with joy because of your partnership in the gospel from the first day until now, being confident of this, that he who began a good work in you will carry it on to completion until the day of Christ Jesus (Phil. 1:3-6, *NIV*).

Paul thanks God for the Philippians. He prays for them with joy. What a joy to let them know of his love for them!

Paul is letting us in on a secret here. Love builds love. Paul loves the Philippian Christians, and so he thanks God for them and has a joyful attitude when he prays for them. These very things contribute further to his love for them. And when he writes so lovingly to them, they can hardly help growing in their love for him!

Is there someone you do not love as much as you could? We all have someone like that in our lives. Try applying Paul's "secret formula" to that person. Thank God for him. Focus on his good qualities (yes, he does have some!). Think about all the reasons you can be thankful for him. Keep it up over the days and weeks, and you will discover that your love is growing.

Need a little more help doing that? Here's a sample. The focus of this prayer is a fellow Christian whose personality irritates the one who is praying:

"Lord, I want to thank you for Joe. Help me to focus on the good things. He comes to church faithfully. (Pause.) He . . .uh . . . studies his Sunday School lesson. He. . .I guess he really loves you, Lord. That's neat. Thank you! And Lord, he brings other guys to our youth meetings and tells them about you. Thank you for that! Thank you that he's friendly to everyone. Thank you that he's reliable. Thank you, Lord, for Joe."

The more you pray with thankfulness and joy for others, the more you will find to be thankful and joyful about. When you cooperate with God, He can do great things with your attitudes.

Being thankful does not mean that you become blind to people's faults. People are only human—and the Christians at Philippi were only human. We all have our failings. We can be critical and unforgiving when someone makes a mistake. We don't always appreciate the efforts others make to teach us spiritually. Some of us can get downright mad. The Philippians must have had their share of all our human failings.

But Paul passed all that sludge through a special filter called love. Because he loved them he chose to stress the good things and to ignore the bad.

Every time the apostle prayed for his Christian friends he recalled something that made him happy and thankful. He didn't waste time and energy rehashing the negative experiences. He preferred to think about their "partnership in the gospel from the first day until now" (v. 5). Perhaps they had helped him teach the Word of God. Maybe they had encouraged him when things weren't going well. It's evident that they had sent a contribution when his funds were low. They had been his partners and he could tell them, "I really miss you. It's great to tell the Lord how much I appreciate you for being *you*."

14

Love's perspective has another facet: It remembers that God finishes what He starts. That truth can help us keep going when we might get discouraged about ourselves or about others. Paul knew that the believers at Philippi were not perfect; but he also knew that the Lord would bring His good work to completion in their lives. Meanwhile, the apostle chose to focus on their strengths.

A Heart-felt Affection

Paul's next statement gives further insight into his feelings for the Philippian believers.

> It is right for me to feel this way about all of you, since I have you in my heart; for whether I am in chains or defending and confirming the gospel, all of you share in God's grace with me. God can testify how I long for all of you with the affection of Christ Jesus (Phil. 1:7,8, NIV).

Let's paraphrase that opening statement. "It's okay for me to have these thoughts about you because I have you in my heart." That implies a warning for all of us. If you have somebody on your mind without having him in your heart, he may end up in your hair—or on your conscience. There is probably no human being in the whole world you couldn't criticize for something if you worked at it hard enough. But if you are not motivated by a loving concern for a person, you have no right making judgments about him. You cannot be objective enough. You can't even be fair. Not unless you see him as a worthwhile person who has as much right as you do to be understood and forgiven and accepted. You should want to do what you can to help him find a little happiness—even if you do not particularly like the guy.

That's what it means to have someone "in your heart."

That kind of attitude was Paul's great leveling tool. Rich or poor, feast or famine, sink or swim, he saw himself as a partner with every other believer. As people who belonged to Christ, they were all in the battle together.

It's a little tricky to adopt that point of view when you take a cold, hard look at other Christians. We're still humans. We can be as difficult as unbelievers. We defend our rights with a passion when someone tramples on them. We lose our temper if we are pushed too far. We make up our mind about who the good and bad guys are and we decide whom we like and dislike. We can be harsh and unforgiving—especially with the bad guys. We learn ways to punish everyone within range when something bugs us.

We act that way because we forget we're all in the same boat. As Christians, we have a common cause—even with the people we disapprove of.

Paul longed for God's best in every Christian's life. That is the stuff Paul's prayer is made of. It is an unselfish prayer and one that remembers the common cause. In our Philippians text, Paul words it like this:

> *And this is my prayer: that your love may abound more and more in knowledge and depth of insight, so that you may be able to discern what is best and may be pure and blameless until the day of Christ, filled with the fruit of righteousness that comes through*

Jesus Christ—to the glory and praise of God (Phil. 1:9-11, *NIV*).

When we talk about Christian love we talk about a love that grows. It's not content to be the same today as it was yesterday. It's designed and constructed to keep moving. There's always a better way to handle a situation. We can work at improving our diplomacy, making people around us feel more comfortable. We can try harder to give a little happiness —even when it seems people don't appreciate or deserve the effort.

Actually, "grow" isn't quite the right word to describe what love is designed to do. Most English translations of the New Testament use the word "abound." That's a word we don't hear very often in conversation, but it packs a lot of meaning. "Plentiful" is a good backup word. But you get a glimpse of the real meaning of "abound" when you look at the Latin word it comes from. *Abundare* means "to flow out from something in waves." That's what Christian love does. It flows like a river at flood stage. It comes from an inexhaustible source down inside—the love of Christ that was planted there when He came to live in our hearts. More and more this love molds our attitudes and actions and makes us a source of happiness to others.

"In knowledge and depth of insight," Paul adds. We don't get very far in loving people if we do not know something about them. And beyond that, even when we get to know what makes them tick, we have to work at understanding how they got to be the way they are. They may have some pressures we don't know anything about. Things may have happened to them along the way that would make us even harder to get along with if they'd happened to us.

We might take an instinctive dislike to someone at first and let that feeling go on 'for years—even for a lifetime. But it's not likely to be that way if we work a little bit at getting to know him. Acquaintance is one thing; *knowing* someone is another. Maybe the person you dislike is the way he is because he needs a friend. Your friendship might make him different.

When we get right down to it, one of the most important factors in our life here on earth is the influence we have on other people. So this love we're concerned about must have an unselfish purpose. It touches people's lives to make them whole and happy. It reaches out with the offer of Christ's love to those who've never heard or never fully understood. It has an aim, and that aim is to do something good for other people.

Christian love sows as it grows. It recognizes the needs all humans have in common. It says to all who come our way, "What Jesus does for me He can do for you. I'd like to be the one to introduce you to that kind of happiness."

That's the happy prayer that opens the happy book that Paul wrote to the Philippians. It's a good prayer, whether voiced for others or for yourself.

PUT IT TO WORK
1. Write down in the fewest possible words what you think the Bible means by the word "love."
2. Can you think of specific situations in which you've demonstrated that kind of love in your

dealings with others? How about the times when you fell flat on your face and acted as if you didn't know what the word "love" means?

3. Paul wrote that everything he remembered about the Christians in Philippi made him happy and thankful. When you think about people in your church you may get some feelings that are not as generous. What was the secret that gave Paul such good thoughts? How could you put that secret to practical use in your own relationships?

2
FUNNY THING HAPPENED ON MY WAY TO JAIL

Things had a way of happening to the apostle Paul —and not always pleasant things at that. Wherever he went he got more than his share of attention. Some considered him famous and others thought him notorious. There were those who loved him and those who hated him, but nobody got away with pretending he wasn't there.

From all we learn by piecing together the evidence, the apostle was a hard man to ignore and a tough act to follow. Not that he wanted it that way. The way the Bible presents the facts, Paul was basically a humble man whose personal theme was "not I, but Christ" (see Gal. 2:20). But he spent most of his time in the limelight. How else could he get the job done that God had assigned him?

People who opposed the gospel singled Paul out for special attention wherever he went. That might seem complimentary from our point of view, but the apostle probably didn't think of it that way. The attention he got from Roman authorities and the Jewish hierarchy usually proved to be bad news, and he already had more than his share of that. The kind of attention he got was the kind a guy could live without!

How Hardships Advanced the Gospel

When you review the record of Paul's hardships you wonder what right the rest of us have to complain about our problems. Second Corinthians tells the story. There were "beatings, imprisonments and riots ... hard work, sleepless nights and hunger" (6:5, *NIV*). And then, a few chapters later (11:23-27), he lays it all on the line:

> *I have worked much harder, been in prison more frequently, been flogged more severely, and been exposed to death again and again. Five times I received from the Jews the forty lashes minus one. Three times I was beaten with rods, once I was stoned, three times I was shipwrecked, I spent a night and a day in the open sea, I have been constantly on the move. I have been in danger from rivers, in danger from bandits, in danger from my own countrymen, in danger from Gentiles; in danger in the city, in danger in the country, in danger at sea; and in danger from false brothers. I have labored and toiled and have often gone*

without sleep; I have known hunger and thirst and have often gone without food; I have been cold and naked (NIV).

It's not hard to imagine someone exclaiming to Paul in undisguised admiration, "Man, there's never a dull moment for a guy like you, is there?!"

Because of his zeal for Christ and his love for people around him, Paul was constantly on the move. He stayed in one place only long enough to win people to Christ and see them established as a group of believers capable of carrying on the work. Then he was off to another place where no one knew about Jesus Christ. He was always in motion.

A moving target may be harder to hit, but it's easier to notice. It appears from the record that Paul was about as noticeable as they come. As a result, a lot of sharpshooters used him for target practice.

So the circumstances are no surprise. As he wrote this letter to the people he had won to Christ in Philippi—Paul was in trouble again. Knowing what he knew about God and people and eternity, he could no more keep quiet than he could sit still. The world he lived in was happier and wealthier because he seldom did either one.

And as a result, things had a way of happening to Paul that kept him leaning hard on the Lord. Not that those "happenings" ever really bothered him. He took them in stride. In his letter to the Philippians, Paul puts it this way:

Now I want you to know, brothers, that what has happened to me has really served to advance the gospel. As a result, it has become clear throughout the whole palace guard and

to everyone else that I am in chains for Christ.
Because of my chains, most of the brothers in
the Lord have been encouraged to speak the
word of God more courageously and fearless-
ly (Phil. 1:12-14, *NIV*).

What had "happened" to Paul began when he was
dragged out of the Jerusalem temple (see Acts 21:30)
and charged with being a troublemaker and sedition-
ist three years or more before he wrote this letter.
After that first episode, he was in and out of court
trials and was the object of near riots for several
months. Then he spent something like two full years
in prison in Caesarea while the authorities tried to
decide what to do with him. Finally he got a hearing
before King Agrippa. Meanwhile, on the basis of his
Roman citizenship, he had appealed to Caesar for a
review of his case. Agrippa sent him on to Rome in
custody of a centurion named Julius.

The group of travelers, including several prisoners
and guards, engaged passage on whatever ships happened to be moving in the general direction of Rome.
The irony of it for Paul was that if he had not appealed to Caesar he would have been freed for lack
of incriminating evidence against him (see Acts 26:
32). A goof on Paul's part? Or was it the unerring
hand of God guiding the apostle to the exact place
and circumstances of His choosing?

Whatever the answer, Paul's "happenings" had
only begun when the group of prisoners headed west.
That voyage to Rome had to be one of the most
action-packed journeys ever recorded (see Acts 27;
28). Head winds, storms at sea, shipwreck, treachery,
cold of winter—even the bite of a poisonous snake

suffered by the apostle on the island of Malta—added to the excitement of the trip to Rome. Few besides Paul expected to survive the series of misfortunes. The party was stranded throughout the winter months, but after a long and uncomfortable experience prisoners and guards alike arrived at the emperor's palace. There Paul was given permission to get a place of his own (see Acts 28:16) and live under the surveillance of soldiers especially assigned to guard the man of God.

That's what "happened" to Paul on his way to writing the letter to the Christians in Philippi. He ended up under house arrest, but it was still a grim situation. Paul was held prisoner in Rome for two years (see Acts 28:30) before he got a hearing.

But Paul wasn't complaining. He knew how to be happy in spite of circumstances—and he was very happy that what had happened to him had "served to advance the gospel."

Paul might have said something like this: "It wasn't a miscarriage of justice or the grinding of the Roman system that put me here. It wasn't King Agrippa or the people who hate me for preaching the gospel. It was God who laid the plans that I should tell kings and rulers about Jesus Christ. It was God who made it happen as it did. Because I trust Him and He loves me, I can be happy in what ought to be a very unhappy situation."

Comfort Is a Low-priority Item

The fact is that Paul's comfort was not of prime importance. God's plan involved getting the gospel to certain people in certain places—and if it required discomfort and inconvenience for His servant, so be it. If comfort and convenience were the goal, *Fox's Book of Martyrs* would never have been written. Heroes of the faith would not have been burned at the stake, beheaded, strangled, starved, thrown in dungeons, stripped of earthly possessions, disgraced, and separated from friends and loved ones. All those little "happenings" can get mighty inconvenient for the lover of comfort and security.

At the top of Paul's list of priorities was something he called "the gospel." He wanted to tell people something crucially important about God. He got his pleasure in life from helping spread the good news about Jesus Christ to people who didn't know Him. His imprisonment gave him an outreach penetrating right into Caesar's palace complex!

Paul had one special privilege that gave a different tone to the entire ordeal. He was allowed to invite the leaders of the Jewish synagogue to his apartment for a bit of spiritual dialogue. Some of these people became believers and some went away enemies, but from that day on a steady stream of inquirers came to Paul to learn about God.

"What has happened to me has really served to advance the gospel," Paul wrote. It was worth the anxiety, discomfort, uncertainty and personal inconvenience he had endured for the past several years. All those experiences were part of the bargain. They had earned for him the right to tell people Christ died for their sins.

The apartment Paul occupied may have been considered a part of Caesar's household. That complex was huge. Some 3000 members of the elite Praetorian

Guard lived there, plus hundreds of other people of all walks of life who made up what Paul calls "Caesar's household" (see Phil. 4:22). What better strategy to reach these people with the gospel than to install Paul within the palace walls? Wherever he went, the gospel message was sure to go.

When Paul first arrived in Rome as a prisoner, he probably was seen in no better light than all the others. But the kind of stuff Christians are made of comes through in due time. It doesn't take an atomic explosion to get people to notice what we stand for. It wasn't long before people in the palace complex began to realize this prisoner from Jerusalem simply was not the criminal type. Thief, murderer, anarchist? Not this loving man. The word began to get around that Paul was a prisoner solely because of his religious beliefs. That made some members of the "household" curious to know what those beliefs were.

"I am in chains for Christ," is the way Paul describes his situation. Whether that meant actual chains or not we've no way of knowing. "I'm all tied up in knots" does not mean literally that I've got a length of rope around me. Maybe "chains" was a way of identifying himself as a prisoner. But we can't forget that Paul was in the hands of a harsh and sometimes cruel system. He may have been literally chained to the soldiers assigned in eight-hour shifts to guard him.

In our culture it may be difficult to identify with someone who is actually in chains because of his faith in Jesus Christ. A person who carries a Bible, cleans up his life and tells others what God has done for him may be branded a religious nut, but no one is going to put handcuffs on him or throw him in jail.

Yet that kind of persecution is not as far away as you might think. Not too long ago in the African nation of Chad, under President Tombalbaye, Christians were persecuted for resisting tribal initiation rites which included drinking blood, sexual indignities, and other unpleasant features. Those who declined to go through with the rites because of their commitment to Christ were mutilated, tortured, and sometimes buried alive.

Buddhists who become Christians are often disowned and cut off by their families. Muslims who become Christians are often in danger of being killed by members of their own family.

In some Communist-dominated countries Christians are often arrested and sent to prison for distributing Christian literature or teaching children about Christ. Children of believers have been taken away from their parents, to be raised in state orphanages away from the "contamination" of Christianity.

There are also subtle ways a really committed Christian here and now may be penalized. Some people think religious freaks who wear a chip on their shoulder probably deserve it. It's possible to ask for trouble and get more than you ask for. But even a thoughtful, loving Christian life can result in a form of persecution.

Becky began to find a lot of personal fulfillment in a Bible study group soon after she became a teenager. Her unbelieving older brother had a friend who asked where she was going one evening as she left the house. "To Bible study," she answered, pausing with her hand on the door knob.

"Oh, good night!" he grimaced. "You really dig Bible study?"

"I sure do," she said.

"And how long do you expect this Christian thing to last?" he asked, sarcasm dripping from each word.

"Forever," Becky answered.

"Forever!" he mocked her with a nasal twang. "Someday you'll grow up, Becky, and find out what life's all about."

Another teenager I know said "thanks but no thanks" to the romantic advances of an arrogant high school senior who apparently thought she'd be a pushover. Hoping to make it an opportunity for personal witness, she told him of her commitment to Jesus Christ. Within a week she learned she'd been nicknamed "Miss Chastity Belt" in the circle of friends he ran around with.

Sue became a Christian as a freshman in high school. Her mother was upset, to say the least. Sue was forbidden to go to church, to talk to Christian friends, or to be away from home except for school until she renounced her new-found faith. She was "imprisoned" in her own home for Christ.

Paul shrugged off persecution as being a relatively unimportant matter. "Chains" held no terror for him —not because he didn't respond to pain and inconvenience like everyone else—he did. He wasn't any more fond of loneliness or rejection than we are. But he knew there would be "chains" when he got involved in living for Christ—and he knew there was a purpose for them. His sufferings were all a part of God's plan. He had no complaint.

And it wasn't long before everyone else knew that,

whatever the mysterious forces at work in his life, Paul was in Rome on business for Someone Else. In a culture where everyone acted in his own interest that unusual fact got people's attention. The people in Caesar's household were ready to listen to the man willing to endure so much for what—and whom—he believed.

And his attitudes got to the Christians too. Somehow his "chains" encouraged the other believers to "speak the word of God more courageously and fearlessly" (Phil. 1:14, *NIV*). It's hard to understand why the imprisonment of the apostle would encourage other Christians to speak out. You'd think it would be just the opposite—they'd be afraid to speak up and take the risk of joining Paul.

Maybe it was the way Paul took his confinement—rejoicing in the Lord and continuing to speak boldly to everyone within earshot. Maybe the others figured, "Here Paul is a prisoner, but he doesn't seem too upset about it. If I witness to others, even if I wind up a prisoner, maybe it won't be so bad."

Or maybe they figured, "If God can use Paul even while he has a Roman soldier chained to him, He can use me when I'm free."

Whatever the explanation, the result was that there was an awful lot of talk around the palace about Jesus Christ of Nazareth.

Christ Is Preached Despite Troublemakers

But not all who talked had pure motives. When we are dealing with humans we can count on human imperfections surfacing sooner or later, and that happened among the Christians in Caesar's household.

Paul describes the problem like this:

> It is true that some preach Christ out of envy
> and rivalry, but others out of good will. The
> latter do so in love, knowing that I am put
> here for the defense of the gospel. The former
> preach Christ out of selfish ambition, not sin-
> cerely, supposing that they can stir up trouble
> for me while I am in chains. But what does
> it matter? The important thing is that in
> every way, whether from false motives or true,
> Christ is preached. And because of this I re-
> joice.
>
> Yes, and I will continue to rejoice, for I know
> that through your prayers and the help given
> by the Spirit of Jesus Christ, what has hap-
> pened to me will turn out for my deliverance
> (Phil. 1:15-19, NIV).

So there was good news and bad news among the
Christians in Rome. They "spoke the word of God
more courageously and fearlessly" because Paul was
there, but not all of them did it for the right reasons.

You mean people can witness for Christ and be
insincere about doing it? Well, check it out—being
sure to begin with a study of your own motives. Any
of us might be guilty of several possibilities for wrong
motivation:

1. Witnessing because my pastor, Sunday School
teacher or youth leader puts the pressure on me.

2. Talking about Jesus because I want to win
someone to my point of view—get a scalp, or cut
another notch in my spiritual six-shooter.

3. Talking about the Lord because we have a mem-
bership drive at the church.

No one knows exactly what motivated the "bad guys" in Paul's particular situation. The "good guys" did what sounds like the right thing under the circumstances. They saw the example Paul set and they responded. They got busy telling others what the world needs to know about Jesus Christ. Their attitude seemed right. They sympathized with Paul, understood his concerns and felt they had a part in what he was doing. They were grateful for his ministry to them. They wanted to help him in return. They acted in love. But it seems we can't say the same thing about the "bad guys."

We don't know exactly what they did, but we do know why they did it—envy, rivalry, selfish ambition, and a desire to stir up trouble for Paul. Not a pretty picture!

Maybe they were doing something like this: they would preach, "God saves all who love Him; He helps them out of all their troubles." This would be a way of degrading Paul since the apostle was in jail, and thus was in trouble; he must not love God or else God would get him out.

Maybe their fault lay in areas indicated by that word "rivalry." Maybe they were competitors for the fame and position that Paul had acquired in his service. They wanted some of the glory, too—though they wouldn't want to suffer as he had suffered or work as hard as he worked! They were competitors. And the Bible doesn't recommend competition or rivalry as worthy motives for telling others about Jesus Christ.

That fault may lurk in the background of a certain amount of Christian "outreach" today. It isn't necessarily deliberately malicious. Most people don't pray for the ruin of another church in order to benefit their own. The competitive spirit certainly is nothing evil in itself, as long as it does not get out of hand. It flavors just about every area of human activity from the Houston Astrodome to the local beauty queen pageant. Any area of achievement you can think of would be a dull scene without a bit of healthy rivalry.

Competition has its place in Christian activities too, but it is an unreliable motive for communicating Christ to other people. Somehow in the case of Paul's disagreeable friends the whole thing degenerated into a program of harassment. Maybe they got carried away with the competitive idea. Whatever went wrong, they ended up "supposing that they can stir up trouble" for Paul through their efforts.

And that's a hard one to analyze. It wasn't a commendable attitude they had, but we can assume that the people Paul wrote about were Christians just the same. It's sad but true that Christians don't always have commendable attitudes. But the fact that what we do or think or feel isn't always up to our own standards does not banish us from God's Kingdom. Our humanity can be counted on to show its true colors now and then in spite of our commitment to Christ. Something got past the spiritual defenses of some of the Christians in Caesar's household, and they responded with behavior unworthy of a child of God.

But notice that Paul does not protest or condemn those people. "It doesn't really matter," he writes, shrugging it off. That does not sound like Paul in a way, because he is usually intolerant of sin—and what they were doing was sin. "Get rid of all bitterness, rage and anger, brawling and slander, along with every form of malice" (Eph. 4:31, *NIV*), he exhorted the Ephesians. But Paul knew that in spite of the high standards placed before Christians, we do fail. In the next verse he urged just as strongly that they practice loving acceptance of each other in spite of their faults: "Be kind and compassionate to one another, forgiving each other, just as in Christ God forgave you" (Eph. 4:32, *NIV*).

So at Rome he practiced what he preached. The reason he could make a concession in this case and not condemn the competitive spirit was that the harm was meant only for him. He was the one privileged to forgive. No one else would be hurt by the envy these people had displayed, so Paul saw it as an insignificant failing. He could take it because, after all, the gospel was being preached. God's program was still in motion. People who needed to know what Christ has done were getting the message.

In effect, Paul says, "Who cares about their motives? What really matters is that Christ is preached. And as far as I'm concerned that's something to be happy about."

That's a remarkably detached point of view. It hardly seems natural—perhaps not even *normal*—for a living, breathing human to take such an attitude. But there it is. With Paul, forgiveness, understanding, and unselfishness were a way of life. They were part of his secret of personal happiness.

So whatever the situation and whoever the culprit, he was able to relax. God was working out the details of His own plan and purpose. It was all safe in His

33

hands. And the apostle knew that the way to happiness was to accept the situation and rest in the Lord.

PUT IT TO WORK

1. If Paul really was a humble and loving man, how can you explain the fact that several times in his life he ended up in jail? Can you conceive of a "good Christian person" being put in jail today because of his faith?

2. Take about 30 minutes to memorize 2 Corinthians 11:23-27. Then recite it back to yourself the next time you feel someone is persecuting you. You may find you have less reason to complain than you think!

3. What do we mean when we talk about things that "happen" to us? If God controls "things" the way Romans 8:28 describes it, can the believer suffer a personal setback that is not a part of God's plan for his life? What should the Christian's attitude be when situations do not turn out the way he wanted or planned?

3
Philippians 1:20-30

I'VE MADE UP MY MIND ABOUT LIVING

You seldom catch Billy Graham speechless. Few men in our day have his gift of eloquence. But several summers ago at a Ft. Lauderdale beach a crowd of college and high school kids just for a moment caught him off guard.

The big Easter bash was just catching on, and someone got the idea for a one-shot Graham crusade on the beach. So there stood the evangelist on a hastily erected wooden platform at the end of Las Olas Boulevard, along with Anita Bryant and a few other big name attractions. Billy's immediate problem was how to get the serious attention of maybe 10,000 teenagers in a very festive mood.

That's when he led with his chin. "What's the one thing that is worth living for today?" Billy asked his audience—mostly sitting or lying on the sand.

"Sex!" some smart guy shouted, almost before anyone else had a chance to think.

"Yeah, sex!" echoed a chorus of voices, followed by waves of raucous laughter. It took several minutes before the evangelist had his crowd—and himself—under control again.

The kids had made their point. Press some people for their reason for living and they have a hard time giving you a good answer. Sex has its good points, but it's scarcely the one thing worth living for. Sex is a popular subject for fantasy, but making those fantasies come true takes skills, relationships and opportunities hard to come by. Sex can be beautiful and fulfilling, but if it were all life had to offer, most people would be better off dead—or never born.

So back to Billy and the beach for a second look at that provocative question: What *is* the one thing worth living for today?

Judging by the soaring suicide rate among teenagers that's a question well worth asking—and answering. Some find no reason at all for living, so they choose death. Yet, for most people death is the biggest question mark of all—the terrifying unknown. For one thing, we're afraid it might be a painful experience. Then there's the problem of what lies beyond. You can take your pick of theories, of course. The choices range from the Indian's "Happy Hunting Ground" to the Buddhist's Nirvana, with a lot of highly imaginative possibilities in between. Or maybe the theory of reincarnation appeals to you. No one's been there to get proof, so you can take your pick. But the fact that we "think" something or "believe" something doesn't mean that's the way it's going to be. Death is whatever death *is*—for *everybody*. It's not one thing for the Indian, another for the reincarnationist and still another for the guy who believes there is no such thing.

The rising rate of suicides among teens doesn't necessarily say death is attractive. It does say that for some people there is a point at which life is no longer worth living. Ugly or fearful as it may be, death to them seems more appealing than life.

Life Is Worth Living

Paul wouldn't have sympathized with the suicide's mind. He found life very much worth living in spite of adversity. But in the proper perspective he also felt death very much worth dying—at least for the person who belongs to Jesus Christ. You can't help being impressed by the enthusiastic way he spells out his philosophy of life and death:

> *I eagerly expect and hope that I will in no way be ashamed, but will have sufficient courage so that now as always Christ will be exalted in my body, whether by life or by death. For to me, to live is Christ and to die is gain* (Phil. 1:20,21, *NIV*).

To die is *gain*? Sometimes when a person is terribly ill and in much pain with an incurable disease, we feel that it is a blessing when he dies. But even that release from suffering is hardly a *gain*. What does Paul mean?

When Paul says death is gain for a Christian he's referring to something positive and wonderful—something only a believer in Jesus Christ can claim.

"Death is gain" means that death is graduation to something even better than life. As Christians we're happy to be alive even when the circumstances get painful. But we are just as happy when it's time to move on up to graduate school. And we can make that statement honestly and sincerely because we know that God has excitement in store for us in eternity. Heaven will be worth waiting for. That's not theory; it's biblical fact!

A great Christian teacher a couple of generations ago put together 365 daily devotionals using Philippians 1:20 as the title for his book. Too long for a title? Well, he didn't use all the words Paul used. He carefully selected just five that tell the whole story: *My Utmost For His Highest* (Dodd, Mead and Co., New York, N.Y.). That's the title of Oswald Chambers' book.

And that was the theme of Paul's life—my utmost for His highest. It was the principal ingredient in his formula for happiness. He did his very best, and he did it for God's glory. The results could be left safely in God's good hands.

You can't make Paul's statement about death, though, unless you share his philosophy of life; "For to me, to live is Christ." He was preoccupied with loving, serving and learning about the Son of God. Psychologists would say Jesus was Paul's "master sentiment." Nothing mattered for the apostle quite as much as the prospect of His "Well done, thou good and faithful servant" (Matt. 25:21, *KJV*).

So if we find it hard to share Paul's "death is gain" sentiments, maybe it's because we lost him back at "to me, to live is Christ." The two thoughts go hand in hand. Until we decide what we're living for, we can't expect to handle the idea of dying.

"For me, to live is _____." You fill in the blank words. Maybe it's being popular, or making good grades, or owning a Kawasaki or a Hobie Cat. Your master sentiment could be money, athletics, pleasure, security, or your reflection in the mirror the first thing every morning. There are dozens of other possibilities. No one knows but you what makes your life worth the effort. You supply the missing words—and keep them to yourself. But if you come up with anything at all but Christ, you won't find it possible to add, "and to die is gain." No one would believe you if you did.

To Live or to Die?

Paul isn't content, though, to let the idea rest quite yet. He really does have a theoretical conflict worth sharing, and he wants to explain it further. Here's the way he spells it out:

> If I am to go on living in the body, this will mean fruitful labor for me. Yet, what shall I choose? I do not know! I am torn between the two: I desire to depart and be with Christ, which is better by far; but it is more necessary for you that I remain in the body. Convinced of this, I know that I will remain, and I will continue with all of you for your progress and joy in the faith, so that through my being with you again your joy in Christ Jesus will overflow on account of me (Phil. 1:22-26, NIV).

When a man finds the prospect of death just as

inviting as the prospect of life, how does he solve his dilemma? Does this mean he is suicidal?

It's not difficult to find the answer if we follow Paul's chain of logic.

To begin with, we need to see that Paul had no real choice. There's no reason to picture him with a gun in his hand, a noose around his neck and a bottle of pills before him, struggling with the idea of taking his own life and making an escape from reality. It's all a theoretical dilemma—much like Hamlet's familiar "To be, or not to be: that is the question!"

All Paul wants is a settled point of view that will satisfy his own great intellect. And that point of view certainly is worth pursuing today.

How should a Christian feel about the "live-or-die" question? Terrified? Unconcerned? Smug?

Finding the right answer begins with outgrowing a your-guess-is-as-good-as-mine mentality. Some well-intentioned person is often around to assure us all religions have more or less the same value. At first it seems an admirable and humble point of view. We should, after all, cultivate tolerance. To feel my religion is true and another's is false seems pretty narrow. Why shouldn't the Hindu be just as good as I am? It's not his fault he was born in India while I was born in "Christian" America.

So we find ourselves right back at the comments on Nirvana and the Happy Hunting Ground. Maybe truth *is* what each person accepts as truth—and who can claim a corner on it? Or maybe the cynic is right who says there's no such thing as truth, especially about God and what happens after we die. Maybe all those answers are right out of the imagination.

Maybe when you are dead you just cease to exist—like a dog, a race horse, a hamster or a goldfish.

From that point of view, though, there is little difference between the "all-truths-equal" and the "no-truth-at-all" ideas. To say all truths have equal value even when they contradict each other, you have to turn off your brain. Two contradicting propositions can't both be true. You can't twist words and bend their meaning quite that far. If truth doesn't exclude *un*truth, then we're left with words that have no meaning at all.

Pontius Pilate traveled an interesting road to reach his cynicism. "What is truth?" he asked Jesus at His mock trial. Pilate was an agnostic and an uneasy religious hypocrite. The political situation he served forced him to worship Caesar and an assortment of Roman gods, but that didn't make him a believer in anything. To him truth was relative and therefore nonexistent. You take your choice based on the advantages. Nothing is definite or final or real.

Pilate's mind seemed closed to any real contact with truth. It's possible to get that cynical even without traveling the road Pilate traveled. We watch religious people and learn their inconsistencies. We discover that Sunday School teachers—even pastors, deacons and elders—are not perfect either. We note that people of apparently equal intelligence and sincerity end up committed to conflicting ideas about God. Some of them reject Him altogether. So as long as we can manage it, we are tempted to forget the whole thing. Any serious question that arises is met with a vacant stare and a shrug. "Truth? What's that? Whose idea of truth are you talking about?"

Is it arrogant to say that the Christian is committed to *God's* idea of truth? That's where it all starts. God's opinion is trustworthy; ours is not. But Pilate had never made God's acquaintance and therefore he was not aware that Truth personified stood before him as the cynical words came out of his mouth. He should have shut up and listened to the answer.

Jesus has "been there" and brought us a report (see John 3:13). He doesn't place His views alongside the views of Mohammed or Confucius with a generous invitation to choose whichever seems the most appealing. He doesn't make "going to heaven" the rough equivalent of merging yourself into Brahma. Jesus presents Himself always as The Truth (see John 14:6). Anything that contradicts that truth is branded a lie (see John 8:44).

It's Better to Live and Serve

Paul stood on the settled fact that when he finished his life here he'd make a quick transition to the presence of the Lord. He had no uncertainty on that score (see 2 Cor. 5:8). His only difficulty was deciding whether he'd prefer to be here serving Christ or there enjoying Him. He was "torn between the two."

But in the Bible portion we are looking at, he thinks it through and makes up his mind. When you stop to think about it, the whole thing reminds you a little bit of the teenager who was asked by a Christian friend if he'd like to go to heaven.

"Nope," he replied promptly and positively.

"Well, you don't want to go to hell, do you?" his buddy asked.

"Nope," he repeated, "I don't want to go anywhere. I'd like to stay right here! " Paul says he'll stay because there's work to be done, and people to be reached with the gospel, the joy of the Lord to be shared. That's the way he can make his greatest contribution to others.

So there's that key again. Paul lived for others, and that commitment brought him happiness—even in frequent unhappy circumstances. He saw the need of serving other people, bringing them joy, bearing their burdens, spreading the gospel. It's time more of us made up our minds about the real purpose of our life on earth!

Live a Life Worthy of the Lord

The first chapter of Philippians closes with a practical bit of advice to the conscientious Christian. It's a word of wisdom that must have carried Paul right on through to his own untimely death.

> *Whatever happens, conduct yourselves in a manner worthy of the gospel of Christ. Then, whether I come and see you or only hear about you in my absence, I will know that you stand firm in one spirit, contending as one man for the faith of the gospel without being frightened in any way by those who oppose you. This is a sign to them that they will be destroyed, but that you will be saved— and that by God. For it has been granted to you on behalf of Christ not only to believe on him, but also to suffer for him, since you are going through the same struggle you saw I had, and now hear that I still have* (Phil. 1:27-30, *NIV*).

We really don't need a lot of laws to help us live consistent Christian lives. In fact, when we start laying down rules to govern people, we make it difficult for them to weather that "whatever happens" storm Paul talks about. Rules and laws seldom allow for those totally unexpected developments that complicate our lives. For example, nobody furnished Paul with a pamphlet full of rules to govern the Christian when he finds himself in jail!

But the apostle does give us a policy statement that can get a Christian safely through practically any circumstances—foreseen or unforeseen. It's an open secret that still applies here and now, though we are separated by thousands of miles and hundreds of years from Paul's situation. *Just do the thing that is worthy of the gospel*, he says.

That gets right down to our basic value system. What is true and what is real? The person who can answer that question with conviction is more likely to handle a tough situation than the person who can't answer. Knowing what is true and real won't guarantee a flawless performance, but it raises the percentage significantly. It takes a little thought and effort, though, to put that proposition to the test.

Paul's overriding commitment was to the truth and reality of something he often calls "the gospel." That gospel can be true and real not only for Paul, but also for everyone else in the whole world. It doesn't matter what language people speak or what life-style they follow or what culture they are a part of. "The gospel" includes all that God offers us in the life, death and resurrection of His Son, Jesus Christ.

Christians can't "stand firm in one spirit, contending as one man" for arbitrary church policies. We would never find ourselves agreeing with all other believers on rituals and fine points of doctrine. Through the centuries churches have found areas of disagreement in forms of government, sacraments, titles, costumes, gestures, taboos, seating arrangements and scores of other fine points. Getting back together again would be like mending Humpty Dumpty with Band Aids. It was a wise man who said, "*What* we believe separates us; *whom* we believe brings us together."

The Bible keeps bringing us back to basic truth and reality. It presents the good news about Jesus and what He offers all who rest their case in His hands. If we settle in on the history and geography and actuality of the gospel, we find motivation to get us over a lot of the hurdles other people never clear. That motivation will serve us especially well when we're misunderstood, opposed or even persecuted. And we will be. Did you notice that Paul talked about "opponents" and about suffering for the sake of Christ?

Being a Christian involves inevitable conflict with the world. A Christian teen who refuses to help a classmate cheat on an exam is in conflict with the world. So is a believer who discovers that every high school party he's invited to is liberally splashed with liquor. And the believer who sees another high schooler steal from a third person is in conflict with the world's ideas that he should keep quiet about it.

Until we decide what we are living for—what's true and what's real—we can't expect to handle the conflicts we run into in the world. But give us the right

45

perspective on what is important and what is not, and we can take care of almost any unexpected development. And we can be happy people while we're doing it. A deep, settled, inner conviction about our goals and purpose in life will give a deep peace and happiness.

PUT IT TO WORK

1. See if you can write out in two or three carefully worded sentences the exact purpose and goal of your life. Resist the temptation to make it what you think someone wants to hear. What is your *real* purpose and goal?

2. Have you ever taken the time to put into words your concept of life after death? Think about it. Read these Scriptures if you need some help: John 14:1-3; Philippians 1:23; 1 Thessalonians 4:15-17; 1 John 3:1-3; Revelation 21:4,5. Suppose a younger brother or sister asked you to describe heaven, or explain what the Christian's experience will be when he dies. Try to express these ideas in phrases that could be understood by a 10-year-old. Then, if you get the chance, try them out on someone about that age.

3. Read 1 Corinthians 15 and think about the concepts of life-after-death expressed there. What does it say is the Christian's chief responsibility while still on this earth?

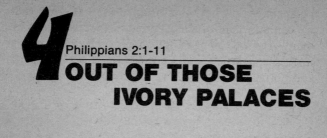

4
Philippians 2:1-11
OUT OF THOSE
IVORY PALACES

The new Christian club on your campus is being torn apart almost before it can get itself together. Some of the members want to have the meetings feature Christian young people and teachers from the high school. What is the answer to this conflict?

Your church basketball team is arguing over who should be the first-string players. How can this conflict be resolved?

Oneness in Christ

The answers are found in some words written by a man who never heard of high school clubs or church basketball teams, but who knew a lot about conflicts and where to find the solutions to them.

> *If you have any encouragement from being united with Christ, if any comfort from his*

love, if any fellowship with the Spirit, if any tenderness and compassion, then make my joy complete by being like-minded, having the same love, being one in spirit and purpose. Do nothing out of selfish ambition or vain conceit, but in humility consider others better than yourselves. Each of you should look not only to your own interests, but also to the interests of others (Phil. 2:1-4, *NIV*).

If we watch for the signals in Paul's letter to the Philippians we get the idea things weren't all sweetness and light in the church. His prayer in 1:9-11 suggests that the believers had a few more things to learn about love, pure purpose and right choices. Later in the letter (4:2), he asks two church personalities named Euodia and Syntyche to bury the hatchet and be friends. Up to then it looked as though they had wanted to bury it in each other's skull!

It seems safe to assume that the little group of believers at Philippi had their share of conflicts, that they fell short a few points in the area of vital Christian living. One of the reasons for Paul's letter was to help them catch up. One of the reasons we study it is that we have some of the same problems they had.

Christians need to be "like-minded." We need to harmonize attitudes and ambitions with others who believe in Jesus Christ. It's something Paul describes as "being one in spirit and purpose."

In fact, that display of unity and love may well test the reality of our total Christian experience.

Dig a little deeper into the idea Paul expresses.

Does being a Christian give you an optimistic outlook on life in general?

Do you really find personal comfort and strength in the fact that Jesus Christ loves you and will love others through you?

Have you experienced the reality of the Holy Spirit living within you?

Does your relationship with Christ make you a more understanding and loving person?

These are questions that stand the test of time amazingly well. Nothing has changed in our sociological or psychological development that makes any of these questions irrelevant today. They stop us right where we are, and demand to know if we're really with it as Christians.

It's seldom comfortable to answer sticky questions about our commitment, but it's rarely unprofitable. It's good to face the facts about our relationship with the Lord—and with other people. If we're right with God, we should be right with God's people. We should even be right with ourselves.

Unity doesn't mean that everyone agrees with everybody else whatever their feelings or convictions. But it does mean being agreeable, even in the face of disagreement. It means respecting other people's opinions as we respect our own.

The young people in a modest-size Michigan church almost discontinued their Sunday evening meetings because of disagreement over the investment of their missions offering. The group was divided about 50-50 between giving the money to a young couple who wanted to serve the Lord in Africa and contributing it to some fine missionaries who had been working for years in Central America.

Finally someone had the bright idea of dividing

into two groups and taking on both projects—even suggesting some friendly competition as to which group could raise the most money for missionary support. They turned a crippling hassle into something positive and productive.

We don't know exactly what got in the way of Euodia and Syntyche's friendship, but it must have been similar to the things that disrupt Christian friendships today. Maybe Euodia suggested a roller skating party and Syntyche held out for a Bible study. Or maybe they couldn't agree on who should have the lead role in the drama presentation. Whatever it was, it seemed important to them at the moment. Their disagreement was causing tension in the church. Paul wanted something done about it—and soon.

A Christian's actions, like any other person's, can be motivated by pride. Our actions and attitudes even as Christians are not above confusion with personal ambition, greed, vengeance or some other unworthy motive.

That's why Paul says, "Do a little self-study and check out the possibilities. When you consider other people better than yourself, you are on the wavelength Jesus Christ has assigned you."

Better than *myself*? You mean, that lamebrain who contradicts me every time I open my mouth in the youth meetings? Or that holier-than-thou creep who wants to spoil everybody else's fun? Are you referring to that great American hero who grabs the credit for everything the rest of us do? Where will I find what it takes to think of people like that as better than me? I don't even *want* to think that way!

In fact, I don't think Paul really means that we should become incapable of discerning weaknesses, either in others or in ourselves. It's not realistic to overlook our own strengths and abilities, either. But Paul's next statement explains his thinking: "Each of you should look not to your own interests, but to the interests of others." He's saying we shouldn't be so wrapped up in loving ourselves and thinking how great we are that we have no time to be concerned about another person. We should be other-centered, not self-centered.

Well! Even that is not easy. It doesn't come naturally to human beings. But it's worth working at—and the Lord will encourage your efforts.

How does this attitude work out in practice? Consider some situations. You're at a party that you've really been looking forward to. You notice a person you barely know sitting in a corner looking lost and lonely. Do you go over and talk to him and try to help him have a good time? Or do you decide just to enjoy yourself with your own friends? What would be the other-centered decision?

You and another girl decide to go out for a snack after school. When you get to the coffee shop your friend discovers that she doesn't have any money with her. You don't have very much money yourself. Do you order a milk shake and let her go without anything; or do you share the money you have so you can both have a Coke?

The whole class has to do a report on a certain topic. You get to the library first and check out one of the most important reference books for that topic. Do you monopolize it until the day before the report is due, or do you work quickly so others can use the book too?

The Mind-set of Heaven

The other-centered attitude is a uniquely Christian point of view. We might call it the "mind-set of heaven." We see it demonstrated in the life of Jesus. From the moment He decided to become a man and suffer the limitations of a human body living on earth, Jesus was giving of Himself for the sake of others (for us!). When we look at Him, we realize how differently things are done in heaven from the way they are done on earth.

What we need, Paul suggests, is to absorb a little of that outlook that characterized the life of Jesus.

> *Your attitude should be the same as that of Christ Jesus:*
>> *Who, being in very nature God,*
>>> *did not consider equality with God*
>>>> *something to be grasped,*
>> *but made himself nothing, taking the very nature of a servant,*
>>> *being made in human likeness.*
>> *And being found in appearance as a man,*
>>> *he humbled himself*
>> *and became obedient to death—*
>>> *even death on a cross!*
>> *Therefore God exalted him to the highest place*
>>> *and gave him the name*
>>>> *that is above every name,*
>>> *that at the name of Jesus*
>>>> *every knee should bow,*
>>>> *in heaven and on earth and under the earth,*

and every tongue confess
that Jesus Christ is Lord,
to the glory of God the Father
(Phil. 2:5-11, *NIV*).

What kind of attitude do we look for in a guy or gal who means business with God? It won't be perfect and it won't always be consistent, but there will be something about that attitude that is patterned after the attitude of Jesus Christ. It will be demonstrated in the things that the person considers important, the things that come first for him, and the way he treats other people.

The *King James Version* uses a word in verse 5 that may give us some additional insight on our "attitude." "Let this *mind* be in you, which was also in Christ Jesus." The mind is where the whole personality is formed. Your decisions are made and your priorities are established in your mind. It's what you think with. So to have the "mind" of Christ we need some input on what and how He thinks about things.

There's plenty of that input in the verses that follow. He "did not consider [think] equality with God something to be grasped, but made himself nothing . . . he humbled himself . . . "

Let's get it clear here and now that Jesus was and is the God of all the universe. It may be a mind-blowing thought, but it's the most important truth of the Bible. Jesus volunteered to step down from that seat of universal power and authority in order to give us something we'll never really deserve.

A few years ago I preached in a fine Bible-believing church in Chicago to a group of people I assumed were well taught in the Scriptures. My text was this "self-emptying" passage about Jesus, and I emphasized the importance of His equality with God the Father.

I stressed the importance of a Saviour who is fully God and who acts with the power and authority of God. After the service, one of those "sweet little old ladies" you hear about got me aside and asked me if I had intended to say that . . . well, that Jesus is God.

"I sure did," I answered. "I don't know of any Bible fact more important."

"Well I've been teaching Sunday School in this church for 25 years," she said, "and I never knew that before."

Twenty-five years a Sunday School teacher in a Bible-believing church, and she never knew that Jesus is God!

He's not some prophet patterned after deity—not some "reasonably accurate facsimile" of the same. As "the Word" He was with God and *was* God (see John 1:1-3), creating the universe for His own purposes (see Col. 1:16). That is the power and the glory that belonged to Jesus when "the Word was made flesh, and dwelt among us" (John 1:14, *KJV*).

Choosing to Serve

But something was more important to Jesus than enjoying that power and glory. So much more important that He laid it all aside for a while to accomplish the higher purpose. This is the point at which we begin to get a glimpse of His mind. The advantages and privileges of being God were all His, and no one could take them from Him. But He could *put them down* if He chose to. And that's just what happens as the full story of the gospel unfolds in Paul's letter. Christ "made himself nothing."

"This is the kind of attitude you ought to have," the apostle writes from his guarded room or from a prison cell in Rome.

But it's easier said than done.

How often do you succeed in putting yourself last? Do you usually consider the welfare of others more important than your own? Well ... half the time? Twenty-five percent? Even 10 percent? If you're like the rest of us it's about as often as gooney birds fly in formation over Puget Sound!

Maybe we can gain some insight if we think a little about why God became a helpless baby on that night in Bethlehem nearly 20 centuries ago. Why did Jesus go that route in humbling Himself? Couldn't He just appear on earth all of a sudden at the age of 33, and then do whatever it took to get us back into contact with God? Why the manger and the "swaddling clothes" and the mother with no one to help her in childbirth?

The answer probably lies in what Jesus came to do. He came to pay the penalty for what we do wrong. He couldn't do that without a complete commitment to being one of us—a human. So Jesus entered the human experience just as we do, by means of a human birth. Having done that, He could leave the human experience only by means of a human death. Nothing else would identify Him with us. Nothing else could save us from our sins.

Jesus had to step voluntarily out of those "ivory palaces." He had to lay aside what it means to be God during 33 years on earth. He exchanged all that for what it means to be man. He was not just *willing*; He *wanted* it that way.

That's the attitude—the mind-set—He offers to share with us. We can learn to have this Christlike attitude if we're really willing to let Him work in us to develop it—and if we're willing to exercise our will to cooperate with Him in the project!

Making Choices

Every time you make a conscious choice to serve others, to set aside some prerogative or right of your own so that another person may benefit, you are developing Christ's attitude.

For example, say you get into a verbal argument with a friend. You have a quicker mind, and you know your friend so well that you could quickly shut him down with a few well-placed remarks. But instead you choose to lay aside that power you have; you lay down your "right" to get even for what your friend said and to show how smart you are. Instead you choose to serve your friend's best interest because you love him. You respond calmly and kindly and the argument cools down.

Your little brother has borrowed your brand-new baseball mitt without asking—and on the very day that you have an important game with your church team. Do you exercise your right to follow your brother to the park and get your new mitt back from him? Or do you let him use it (leaving you with your crummy old mitt) because you love him and you know that he is afraid of the ball and took your mitt to give himself courage?

In your family of seven, the rule is that each person

gets to decide what to watch on television on a particular night of the week. Today your younger sister comes home with the news that her teacher has assigned her class to watch a documentary that will be shown twice during the week. Your sister wants to watch it on your TV night, because the other showing will be on the night she's going to a pajama party at a friend's house. Do you exercise your right to watch a show you've really been looking forward to on your night or can you lovingly give way to your sister's request because you care about her?

Every day we face choices like these. In our choosing, our exercise of our will, we shape our character. If we choose to follow Christ, He will honor our efforts and help us become more and more like Himself. He will help us to see things from His perspective. He came all the way "down from His glory." Compared with that self-emptying of God Himself, any step we take in giving up our rights and privileges seems pretty insignificant!

PUT IT TO WORK

1. Name three situations that happened recently in which you had a choice to exercise your rights or to exercise the mind of Christ. What did you choose? Will you ask God to help you exercise the mind of Christ next time?

2. Try a little exercise in meditation. Read Philippians 2:5-11 over several times. As you do, think about the glory Christ knew in heaven. Bring in everything you can think of about heaven and the presence of the Father—enjoying a sinless envi-

ronment and the limitless bliss of eternity. Contrast that to a role that Christ willingly took up as a human being—the limitations of the human body, a hunger, tiredness, sweat, rubbing shoulders with sinful people, and so on. Praise the Lord for His great love and willingness to do that for you!

3. Be sure you can answer clearly, confidently and without qualification the question, "Is Jesus God?"

5

SMILE, SOMEONE IS WATCHING

A teenager named Eddie had an unhappy adventure. He had a learner's permit but not a driver's license, and so he wasn't allowed to drive his parents' cars unless one of them was with him. He had no problem with that restriction since his parents were around to make sure he stuck to it.

But one weekend Eddie's parents went out of town and left him home alone. Temptation whispered in his ear. It tantalized him with the thought of the car left in the driveway and the key hanging on a hook inside the kitchen door. He toyed with the temptation; he wouldn't drive the car very far, and he could always put in a couple of gallons of gasoline to cover up. No one need know about his harmless little adventure.

But Eddie hadn't counted on running a stop sign with the car loaded down with his friends. And he especially hadn't counted on the local police watching that particular stop sign on that particular afternoon.

Where would you find a policeman willing to overlook a little driving-without-a-license incident? Not in Eddie's hometown. And how do you put in a court appearance and handle a 50-dollar fine without your parents finding out? You don't! So Eddie ended up in big trouble. So much trouble that he figured his "harmless little adventure" wasn't worth it. He wished that he had obeyed his parents not only when they were home but also when they were absent.

When Do You Obey?

We all need to learn the lesson Eddie learned. Some of us learn sooner than others. The Christians at Philippi had learned it, for Paul could write to them,

> Therefore, my dear friends, as you have always obeyed—not only in my presence, but now much more in my absence—continue to work out your salvation with fear and trembling, for it is God who works in you to will and do what pleases him (Phil. 2:12,13, NIV).

Paul had a special relationship with the Philippian Christians. It dated back to the special circumstances in which the church was born (see Acts 16). His letter indicates a very special mutual love and respect. He scolded the Galatian Christians for letting someone deceive them with false doctrines. He condemned the

Corinthian Christians for failing to deal with a gross sin within the church family. But he has no such rebuke for the Christians in Philippi. From the beginning of his letter Paul expresses gratitude and affection for the believers in that city (see Phil. 1:3-8).

That doesn't mean they were perfect, because they weren't. They had to struggle with the same kind of faults and failings we struggle with today. But apparently they *purposed* to obey the Lord, and did their very best to achieve that goal. They intended to let God work out His plan and complete His program in their lives.

Obedience to the Lord had high priority with the Christians at Philippi, even when Paul wasn't there to keep an eye on them. In fact, judging by his comment in verse 12, the apostle felt that's the kind of obedience which counts with God. It's commendable to "walk the straight and narrow" while someone is there to check us out. It's even better to do what's right because of a deep conviction down inside.

That's the kind of obedience God is looking for. He doesn't get His business done through people who follow Christ only when someone in authority is there to ride herd. If I'm one kind of person when my pastor or my parents are watching and another when they're not, guess which kind of person is the real me!

The way to find out what I'm really made of is to watch what I do when I'm free to do whatever I please.

That fact is shown in an interesting development among the Israelites at the close of the book of Joshua.

"We choose the Lord!" the people answered when

61

the aging Joshua warned them against spiritual fence-straddling. "Decide today whom you will obey," he had insisted.

So they made their choice—with their leader there to press them for a decision.

> *"You have heard yourselves say it," Joshua said—"you have chosen to obey the Lord." "Yes," they replied, "we are witnesses." "All right," he said, "then you must destroy all the idols you now own, and you must obey the Lord God of Israel."*
>
> *The people replied to Joshua, "Yes, we will worship and obey the Lord alone."*
>
> *So Joshua made a covenant with them . . . committing them to a permanent and binding contract between themselves and God . . . . Then Joshua sent the people away to their own sections of the country. Soon after this he died at the age of 110* (Josh. 24:22-25,28,29, *TLB*).

All of which has a very encouraging sound. It gives you high hopes that the people finally meant business with God. In fact, you are so optimistic that you have to look twice before you notice that verse 31 in the same chapter contains more bad news than good.

"Israel obeyed the Lord throughout the lifetimes of Joshua and the other old men who had personally witnessed the amazing deeds which the Lord had done for Israel" (Josh. 24:31, *TLB*).

Great! The whole nation made a commitment to obey God. And they kept their promise—as long as Joshua and a few other older men were around to check up on them! Obviously the contract they made was not with God but with the people who were riding herd on them. They had no motivation beyond pleasing Joshua and the men they recognized as leaders.

But the Philippians were different. They obeyed God when Paul was there; and their performance was just as good when he wasn't. Their obedience wasn't based on human surveillance. The Christians at Philippi wanted God's approval at least as much as they wanted Paul's. That gave them a solid basis for a life-style and value system that served them well in the clinches.

Someone Is Watching

When you really love God and want to honor and please Him with your life, it's not too hard to live as if someone were watching you. You know that He *is*.

And you can be sure that others are watching you, too. The believer in Christ lives to some degree in the public eye. The more definite and positive your profession of faith, the more carefully people will watch your every move. There are two reasons for that—one good and one not so good.

The good reason is that people watch the way a Christian handles himself because they'd honestly like to find out what he has that they've missed. Way down inside they have a hunger for something to unravel the mysteries of life. They're impressed by what they see when a real Christian comes along. If there's some possibility that they can get in on what he has, they'd like to give it a whirl.

The not-so-good reason that other people watch Christians is that they're hoping to catch them in inconsistencies. Nothing makes them so happy as to learn that a prominent Christian businessman cheated on his income tax, or a choir leader ran off with an organist. They've already decided church people are hypocrites and the more proof they find the better they like it. These make the most dedicated "Christian watchers" of all. It's a bad day when they fail to catch some church person in something that appears to contradict his claim to be God's child.

It doesn't really matter which class of watchers we're dealing with. It's still a good idea for the Christian to make frequent checks on things in his life that might seem contradictions.

Just as a child's growth is measured on a wall chart, so does the Christian's spiritual growth need to be measured at regular intervals. You are saved by the grace of God, and no amount of work or good behavior on your part qualifies you as a Christian. But once you've become a Christian you find some hard work is waiting to be done. This is not to secure or to insure your acceptance with God. It's to help you grow—to accomplish the things God has for you to do.

Paul calls this "working out" our salvation. Not working it *in*—that's already done. Working it *out* is the term for buying up our options as Christians. It means cooperating with God so He can accomplish His purposes through our lives.

The way God works in us and through us is one of the deep mysteries of the Christian life. There are lots of different methods of doing the job for God. But every person who seeks to do the will of the Lord can claim that God actually works in and through him (see 1 Cor. 12:6).

God Is at Work

This does not make the Christian infallible. He makes mistakes like anyone else, but he does his best and wants to please the Lord. His judgment may be no better than the ideas of a dozen other Christians who disagree with him. But after all is said and done, mistakes and all, he can fall back on the realization that God is at work. He doesn't claim to understand all about it. He can't always explain to others how it works. But it takes a big load off his back to know that in due time God will make everything come out the way He planned it.

> *Do everything without complaining or arguing, so that you may become blameless and pure, children of God without fault in a crooked and depraved generation, in which you shine like stars in the universe as you hold out the word of life—in order that I may boast on the day of Christ that I did not run or labor for nothing. But even if I am being poured out like a drink offering on the sacrifice and service coming from your faith, I am glad and rejoice with all of you. So you too should be glad and rejoice with me* (Phil. 2:14-18, *NIV*).

Can you see Paul's formula for happiness even in circumstances that may seem unhappy? Do your best, and accept full responsibility for your decisions and actions. But don't sweat it when things fail to work out the way you'd hoped.

No complaints and no arguments. Paul is firm about that. After all, if God is at work in us "to will and to do what pleases him," we have no room to complain. And certainly we have no one to argue with. So we accept what is. At least, that's the way it's supposed to work.

Most humans fit into one of two basic categories. There are "how-others-affect-me" people and there are "how-I-influence-others" people. The book of Philippians places a lot of value on the second point of view. The person concerned with favorably influencing others is likely to experience a generous share of happiness. The person mainly concerned about what other people are doing to him—or not doing *for* him—stands a good chance of making himself miserable.

A teenager named Sue traveled across the nation to the troubled community of Watts to take part in the work of a Christian ministry to underprivileged urban people. As she began to get involved in the lives of black kids, she found herself drawn to a little girl with a disfigured left hand. Several years before, the girl's mother had spilled a pan of boiling water on the hand and the family didn't have enough money for expensive medical care and burn therapy.

Sue found the girl tragically withdrawn, unwilling to participate in activities planned for the ghetto kids. The hand was undoubtedly the reason. "It looked like something out of a horror movie," Sue said.

Sue kept trying to establish a friendship with the girl, going out of her way to get past that barrier. But the disfigured girl still kept her distance, just as she did from everyone else.

Then the breakthrough came. One day Sue was standing next to the girl with a group of other young people. Out of the corner of her eye she saw that maimed left hand reaching toward her, then felt the touch of that scar tissue on her arm. Instinctively, she felt an impulse to draw away. But with that instinct she also experienced something else. "This is my test," Sue thought. "In fact, it's the answer to my prayers." So she flashed an understanding smile to the little girl and took that scarred and twisted hand gently in her own.

From that moment on, the barrier was down. For the first time since the shocking experience of her burn, the little girl felt accepted. Sue was her friend. She could trust her. And from that moment on Sue found it easy to teach her how God's love reaches out to us in Jesus Christ.

"You shine like stars in the universe," Paul writes. In the eyes of at least one lonely little black girl, Sue was shining. There are ways all of us can take our turn in the same role.

So much in our world is selfish, unfeeling, unloving and unfair that we attract attention any time we break the human tradition of unconcern for others. Some-one is watching. Someone is hoping we'll turn out to be truly different from the rest. Someone wants to "reach for the stars" the same way the little girl in Watts reached out to touch Sue's arm.

That kind of concern for others is the way we "hold out the word of life." It's "practicing what we preach." It's living the Christian life in a way that attracts the attention of others—not to our own good-ness, but to the One who makes it possible for us to love.

Soon after I became a Christian as a young busi-nessman I designed a sign to go in front of the church

I attended. It gave the name of the church and the times of its services, and then it showed a hand holding out a Bible with a part of Philippians 2:16 as the text. It looked like this:

"...holding forth BIBLE the Word of Life"

Christians are responsible to give the Word of God to others, and the Bible is the Word of God. In that sense we can be pictured as hands holding out the Bible, teaching others, urging others to follow Christ. It would be great if more Christians shared the message of the Bible that way.

But when Paul wrote that phrase, "holding forth the word of life," Christians couldn't offer people the Bible as we know it. There wasn't any New Testament at all. The Jewish nation had the Old Testament Scriptures, but they were available in the form of parchment scrolls that were kept at the synagogues.

The Christians at Philippi couldn't go around handing those scrolls to people. There probably were no such scrolls in all of Macedonia anyway—and few people able to read them.

Living the Word of Life

So Paul had some other concept in mind. The Word of Life is not something we hold out in our hand to others. It is something we live. People see it in us and experience it through us. When we show people something that attracts them to Jesus Christ we are doing what Paul teaches here.

That's something we can't fake. We can't say, "Okay, now I'll hold forth the Word by doing a couple of kind deeds." We can't set aside one day a month to be unselfish and loving.

"Hey, is this the first of the month? I'm not supposed to yell at my old man today. I'm supposed to be unselfish and loving. I'll have to work at that."

"Oops, I did it again. Today I'm showing everybody what it means to be unselfish and loving. Why'd I have to lie about the girl I'm taking out tonight?"

"Oh yes, I forgot. This is my unselfish and loving day. I shouldn't have ripped off that eight-track tape from the store. I should have done that yesterday—or waited until tomorrow."

That's just not the way it works. Holding forth the Word of Life in the way Paul meant it is a full-time proposition. It's a growing experience. We are taught by our mistakes and encouraged by our successes. But most of all, we have to believe that sharing Christ with others is God's plan for a useful and meaningful Christian life. It's not only the best way to get happiness—it's also the best way to give happiness to others.

Paul's feelings on that subject are directly related to his strong emphasis on the value of self-sacrifice (see Rom. 12:1,2). Jesus sets the example for selfless service. Inspired by the Holy Spirit, Paul writes that the Christian does not really own himself anymore (see 1 Cor. 6:19,20). It doesn't really matter how he comes out in any given situation. The important thing is that other people are brought into contact with God.

So Paul compares himself with the "drink offering" poured out around the altar in the ancient Jewish sacrifice. It was wine or water apparently wasted, but wasted in obedience to God's demands.

"I am glad and rejoice with you all," Paul writes. You get the feeling he really means it. "So you too should be glad and rejoice with me."

PUT IT TO WORK

1. Explain in your own words why you feel some people are able to act like Christians under almost any circumstances—whether they are being watched or not—and others can't seem to cut it unless someone in authority has an eye on them.

2. Imagine you are a member of the Jewish nation during Joshua's lifetime. You've been taught all of God's rules and regulations for His people, and you're working hard at obeying them. But one by one, Joshua and the other aged spiritual leaders begin to die off. Honestly, what difference do you feel that would make in the way you handled your spiritual responsibilities?

3. Memorize 1 Corinthians 6:19,20. Can you think of any specific attitude you have that contradicts the trust these verses teach?

6

FRIENDS MAKE IT ALL WORTHWHILE

What do your friends mean to you? Have you ever thought about it? Take some time right now to think about your best friend—or your two or three or four best friends—and to consider how your life is richer and better because of them. Isn't it great that God gives us friends?

Paul enjoyed a special friendship with a young man named Timothy. The attachment had nothing to do with age, since possibly as much as 40 years separated them. Paul was a Jew from Tarsus. Timothy was a half-Greek from Lystra. But you can sense the special relationship they enjoyed in the special way Paul wrote about his friend.

I hope in the Lord Jesus to send Timothy to

*you soon, that I also may be cheered when I
receive news about you. I have no one else like
him, who takes a genuine interest in your
welfare. For everyone looks out for his own
interests, not those of Jesus Christ. But you
know that Timothy has proved himself, because as a son with his father he has served
with me in the work of the gospel. I hope,
therefore, to send him as soon as I see how
things go with me. And I am confident in the
Lord that I myself will come soon* (Phil. 2:19-
24, *NIV*).

Timothy was Proverbs 18:24 in action—"a friend
who sticks closer than a brother" (*TLB*)! No "fair-
weather" friendship for him. His commitment to Paul
didn't shift with the wind, tide or sand of circumstances. It was an established fact that didn't depend
on some preconceived idea of how a friend ought to
treat you. The embattled apostle knew he could count
on Timothy's friendship and that's the reason he
wrote as he did. Timothy's friendship contributed to
the apostle's happiness—not just because Timothy
was Paul's friend, but because he shared the apostle's
love for other believers.

The Christians at Philippi were well acquainted
with Timothy. Paul probably led him to faith in
Christ on one of his trips through Lystra, for he calls
him "my true son in the faith" (1 Tim. 1:2, *NIV*). The
new convert then accepted the apostle's invitation to
join his evangelistic team. Can you imagine how
you'd feel if a missionary on his way to, say, Nepal
asked you to come along—with no promises about a
steady income? Timothy must have been the adven-

turesome type, with more than the average share of faith. He accepted, and off they went to find out where the Lord would have them go from there.

That's when the well-known "Macedonian call" came to Paul, directing his party across the Hellespont at the northern end of the Aegean Sea and into the city of Philippi (see Acts 16:9-12). There Timothy worked with Paul and Silas to establish a church. When the two older men ended up in jail, their young assistant Timothy probably assumed both the teaching and the administrative responsibilities in the Philippian church. Thessalonica, Berea, Athens, Corinth and Ephesus were on their schedule after the jail experience, and Timothy probably spent the next several years helping the apostle, obeying his orders, following his example and learning from his teaching.

Through the friendship with Paul, Timothy was growing spiritually and learning to assume responsibility. When Paul decided to return to Jerusalem, he sent Timothy back to Philippi to take over pastoral duties.

It's Not All Sweetness and Light

Would you expect a friendship like that to involve only sunshine, sugar and smiles? That seems unlikely —given the blunt and persistent way Paul had of expressing his views and urging people to faith and faithfulness. There must have been cloudy days, some vinegar and a few frowns in Timothy's learning experience. Paul was interested more in results than in diplomacy, as Barnabas and John Mark discovered when they settled their differences with the apostle by going separate ways (see Acts 15:36-41). Paul had

73

a mind of his own and a fierce determination to do things God's way, no matter how loud the objections.

The record in Acts doesn't include the deep waters these friends passed through when the learning process got sticky, but it's a safe guess there were painful moments and frustrations on both sides. But real friendship can take setbacks in stride. In fact, it will be stronger because of such muscle-building exercises.

"With friends like that, who needs enemies?" Benji complained when the other offensive halfback on his high school team told the coach Benji was consistently breaking training rules and bragging about it to all his buddies. His friend felt that Benji's "cheating" had something to do with his having a rushing average of only 1.8 yards and the fact that the team was two for five so far that season in games. But Benji called it ratting, and did everything he could to make things tough for his teammate.

Later on though, Benji realized that he deserved being "ratted" on. He saw that he was hurting himself and his team, and that his teammate proved a better friend by talking than he would have been by keeping silent.

To Grow a Friendship

Building a friendship takes some work. It doesn't happen automatically. But it's worth the effort. The Christian life is a lonely existence for someone unwilling to work at developing friendships.

Diane had just started her senior year in high school when she discovered what it means to be a Christian. A girl who teamed up with her in a gym class told her the full importance of Christ's death. Then one day she knelt in her bedroom and invited Jesus to come into her heart and make her life worthwhile.

But as far back as she could remember Diane had felt very little need for other people. She was a loner. She liked to do things her own way and didn't want to run the risk of getting involved in other people's lives. As a new believer she saw no reason to change that point of view. When other Christian kids invited her to go to the state park for a cookout she told them there was something else she had to do that afternoon. The church her gym partner attended had an active youth group, but Diane rarely worked up any enthusiasm for the program. Bike riders, volunteer work programs, action groups, school prayer meetings, car washes, neighborhood surveys, all left her cold. Whenever the social chairman called to tell her about an event the kids were planning it generated about as much enthusiasm as a January swim party at Iceberg Point.

And Sunday School she could do without. She claimed the kids weren't friendly. They were nice only to the other guys and gals who had attended that church for years. They smiled at her and said "Glad you're here" now and then, but she could tell they didn't really mean it. The smile was pasted on. If they didn't care to be nice to her, she certainly wasn't going to go out of her way to be nice to them. She'd rather spend Sunday morning at home anyway, amusing herself by flicking the TV set from one gospel program to another.

So it wasn't long before Diane began to wonder if

anything had really happened when she asked Jesus into her life. She didn't grow spiritually, and worse than that it soon stopped bothering her that she didn't. She badly needed Christian friends to share and add meaning to her new discoveries about God. But she wasn't willing to be a friend, so she didn't *make* friends. She never experienced true happiness that comes from building solid Christian friendships.

If you feel that others aren't friendly, there's a good chance the fault lies in your own attitude.

Timothy's attitude was right, and because of that his spiritual life grew and his friendships blossomed. "I have no one else like him, who takes a genuine interest in your welfare," Paul wrote about his "son" and friend in Christ. Having that kind of support during his season of suffering probably made the difference for Paul between coping and not coping in a very bad situation.

The honest offer of your friendship could make the difference between victory and defeat for someone involved in a personal crisis. Can you see how the investment of a bit of time, effort and creativity can be eternally worthwhile?

Humans don't naturally go around offering friendship to people of unknown pedigree. Something new and different has to happen inside us before we're willing to take that risk. But it's one of the risks involved in enjoying the kind of Christian life Paul and Timothy experienced.

It's too bad believers don't take more risks like that. Paul says Timothy was a rare breed—and there certainly weren't many like Paul. They were men of single purpose, and that purpose molded their remarkable friendship. The world surely could use a few more people with that kind of commitment to the Kingdom of God!

The last surviving five-star general from World War II voiced similar sentiments when he summed up his thoughts about the failure of our modern society.

"We have too many men of science, too few men of God," General of the Armies Omar Bradley said. "We have grasped the mystery of the atom, and rejected the Sermon on the Mount. The world has achieved brilliance without wisdom, power without conscience. Ours is a world of nuclear giants and ethical infants."[1]

Anybody for a serious effort to grow up?

Fortunately for Paul, his personal world was populated with an encouraging number of spiritually mature people. And he left us with enough information about them to help us understand how our own value system might work better.

Friend Epaphroditus

Another of those helpful friends was a man not often mentioned in the New Testament. He was known by the Greek name, Epaphroditus.

But I think it is necessary to send back to you Epaphroditus, my brother, fellow worker and fellow soldier, who is also your messenger, whom you sent to take care of my needs. For he longs for all of you and is distressed because you heard he was ill. Indeed he was ill, and almost died. But God had mercy on him, and not on him only but also on me, to spare me sorrow upon sorrow. Therefore I am all the more eager to send him, so that when you see him again you may be glad and I may have less anxiety. Welcome him in the Lord with great joy, and honor men like him, because he almost died for the work of Christ, risking his life to make up for the help you could not give me (Phil. 2:25-30, *NIV*).

Paul hoped to send Timothy to Philippi when the time was ripe, but he thought it *necessary* to send Epaphroditus right away. For one thing, someone had to carry his letter back to the church. In those days they didn't stick on a stamp and drop the envelope in a mail box. They entrusted letters to travelers and hoped they'd survive the trip and remember to make the delivery at the other end. In this case, Epaphroditus was selected for the job.

He had good qualifications. Paul thought of him as a brother, a fellow worker and a fellow soldier. Each role had its own importance. And to the Philippians he was a man with a message.

It's interesting that the Greek word for "messenger" is *apostolos*, which might indicate that Epaphroditus was a traveling evangelist, serving as God's messenger or apostle. Some students of church history feel he may have been the bishop of Philippi.

In any event, Epaphroditus was a citizen of that Macedonian city—a man with the complete confidence of the church there. His hometown Christians had collected a substantial offering to help with Paul's expenses, and dispatched Epaphroditus to deliver the money in Rome. They trusted him completely, and their confidence was well placed.

Now Paul was sending him back, but not with money because the tentmaker had little of that. What Paul did have, however, he was always ready to share. He sent them a word from God on the important subject of finding happiness in all situations no matter what. He had been through good and bad circumstances and found happiness. He had been there. He knew about it from personal experience.

Paul was one of those who "spoke from God as they were carried along by the Holy Spirit" (2 Pet. 1:21, *NIV*). God's Word was the gift Paul entrusted to Epaphroditus on his long and hazardous journey back to Philippi. The same gift is available to us today through the book we call the Bible.

But there's more to Epaphroditus than just his service as a messenger. If he'd been nothing more than a clean-living pony express rider he'd never have rated these six verses at the heart of the book of Philippians. He had something few Christians have these days—something based on the same kind of friendship Paul and Timothy enjoyed. And in the case of Epaphroditus the friendship was directed toward all the other believers in Philippi.

The Interests of Others

"Each of you should look not only to your own interests, but also to the interests of others," Paul wrote in verse 4 of this chapter. There are different ways to put that philosophy into practice, and the situation Epaphroditus finds himself in is one of many possibilities. But it's close to home for some of us.

The trip overland from Philippi to Rome was long,

hard and full of danger. Yet Epaphroditus had taken the trouble and the risk gladly in order to get that offering into Paul's hands at a time of special need. He found happiness in serving God by serving one of God's servants. But somewhere along the way he had contracted a disease or an infection.

Maybe it was caused by overexertion, lack of rest and improper nourishment. It could have been the result of bad weather and inadequate shelter. There was no aspirin or cough medicine in those days—not even decongestants to reduce the symptoms of a head cold. Medical people didn't know about germs in those days. They had no way of knowing how disease and infection were transmitted, much less how to go about treating them.

So when Epaphroditus got sick he was in real trouble. If there were physicians to treat him at all, they probably mumbled something about a bad liver and told him to get plenty of rest and stay out of the night air. The fact is, he almost died. It was the grace of God that spared him. From the way Paul describes his condition it must have been touch and go for a while. There were no hospitals, no clinics and no drug stores. There weren't even any thermometers to tell how high his fever went. Anyone who got sick in those days had to tough it out and hope for the best.

A great situation for getting some sympathy, wouldn't you say? We'd probably play the role as if an Oscar were at stake—groans, sighs, trembling, and all the rest. We'd want flowers, cards, telephone calls and delegations to sit on the bed and tell us how awful we must feel. If all those sympathetic people didn't know we were sick we'd probably pout until they did.

But none of that for Epaphroditus. He had something special, and this was the right kind of situation in which to put it to use. We'd be distressed if our friends *didn't* hear we were sick; Epaphroditus was distressed because they *did*.

That sickness brings up an interesting question, incidentally. Paul had the gift of healing. When he was shipwrecked on the island of Malta he prayed for a man suffering from fever and dysentery, laid hands on him and healed him (see Acts 28:8). This was a man in whom he had no special interest, except that the man's son, Publius, had offered hospitality to Paul and his party. On the other hand, Epaphroditus was a brother in Christ and a valued member of the team. Yet Paul says nothing about healing him. Did he try? Could he have forgotten to pray and lay hands on him and ask God to stop the fever?

Epaphroditus lived "for the work of Christ." Yet the outcome of his illness was in serious doubt for a while. Apparently healing took place according to the will of God, not the will of the healer. There were reasons for the sickness that Paul wasn't aware of.

The Best of Friends

That's the climate God's servants lived in when the church was young. When the elders in Jerusalem sent Judas and Silas with Paul and Barnabas to Antioch they wrote a letter introducing them as "men who have risked their lives for the name of our Lord Jesus Christ" (Acts 15:26, *NIV*). They weren't super heroes. They were ordinary people with weaknesses and doubts just like our own, but they had made up their minds about Christ. They went wherever God

81

led them and were available whenever there was a need.

Probably there was little time for petty grievances and bickering. Sharing hardships helped build lasting friendships. They had a common cause that was bigger than their personal differences. They found happiness together in the service of the Lord.

"However, I consider my life worth nothing to me, if only I may finish the race and complete the task the Lord Jesus has given me—the task of testifying to the gospel of God's grace" (Acts 20:24, *NIV*). That's the way Paul expresses his commitment. You can count on the friendship of a guy who feels that way about it!

PUT IT TO WORK

1. Have you been considering your definition of friendship? What does it mean to you to have a friend? To be a friend?
2. Can you be counted on as a real friend? Do you consider the interests of your friends as important as your own?
3. What have you learned about friendship from your friends? Perhaps you've seen how Joe always listens intently when someone talks to him; or how Sandra rejoices over your joys as much as you do; or how Bill is always ready to help when you need it; or how Kathy is quick to let you know she cares when you have a problem. Make a list of special things you have learned about friendship from your friends. Ask the Lord to help you put these into practice in your own life. And tell your

friends "thank you" for being the way they are!
4. How do your friends affect your service for the Lord? How do you affect your Christian friends' service? What impact are you having on friends who don't know the Lord?

Footnote

1. Sherwood Eliot Wirt, and Kersten Beckstrom, eds., *Living Quotations for Christians* (New York: Harper & Row, Publishers, 1974), p. 215.

7

Philippians 3:1-6

DO GOOD GUYS GET TO HEAVEN?

It begins to dawn on you after a while that Paul emphasizes his teaching by repeating himself. He makes effective use of that threefold rule of good advertising: repetition, repetition, repetition.

Repetition never was boring for Paul. He repeated himself frequently in his writings because he felt the repetition added an extra margin of safety for his readers. And in the book of Philippians the apostle pounds away on two important truths that seem worth a lot of repeating.

One is the basic statement of the entire book: A Christian ought to find happiness in the fact that he knows the Lord. The second is a warning against people who would mislead us with doctrines that don't square with the truth.

But the moment we speak of false doctrines I can imagine a voice in the balcony asking, "Who decides which doctrines are false and which are true?" Someone else may be asking, "What does 'doctrine' mean anyway?"

Christian commitment begins with the idea that the Bible is the Word of God. No mere man has either the privilege or the responsibility of saying what is true and what is not. God does not designate people or institutions to tell others what they may or may not believe. Men and institutions can't be trusted with that kind of authority. So God put His truth in a book and tied it in with the lives of those who trusted Him in the Old and the New Testaments. He perpetuated His truth with quill and parchment, paper and printer's ink. He used the godliness, the experience and the literary style of 44 different writers to put His will and wisdom in written form. He put a book in our hands so we'd avoid the pitfalls of church rules, men's opinions and oral traditions.

It is true, of course, that the Bible is subject to interpretation in many things. Good men differ in their views of some of its teachings. But in its basic doctrines the Bible gives us specific teachings about God's character, about man's needs and about the saving work of Jesus Christ. These facts about God and His relationship with men are the starting point for our understanding of all other doctrines. Paul says it is tremendously important for us to learn our doctrines from God and not from men.

Watch Out for False Doctrine
It is so important the apostle repeats himself often

on that particular theme. He made this warning the subject of the whole book of Galatians (see Gal. 1:8, 9). In the letter to the Philippians he uses the harshest terms to renounce people peddling false doctrines. They are hungry dogs, out to eat up those who accept their unbiblical teachings.

> *Finally, my brothers, rejoice in the Lord! It is no trouble for me to write the same things to you again, and it is a safeguard for you. Watch out for those dogs, those men who do evil, those mutilators of the flesh. For it is we who are the circumcision, we who worship by the Spirit of God, who glory in Christ Jesus, and who put no confidence in the flesh— though I myself have reasons for such confidence* (Phil. 3:1-4, *NIV*).

"Finally," he writes—and a total of 44 verses follow before the letter is finished. In fact, that word "finally" is located at the geographical center of the epistle. As much remains as has gone before.

But Paul may mean that "finally" as a summary of all he's been writing about. A sort of "in the final analysis . . . " type statement. "After all is said and done, the Christian should rejoice in the Lord."

And we should. That much is plain in the doctrines of the Bible. We really can be happy as believers in Jesus Christ, even in the face of threatening circumstances. Rejoice, rejoice, rejoice!

But while you're rejoicing, be on the alert against false teachers who clutter your mind with ideas contrary to the teachings of the Bible. They are "men who do evil." And because the evil they do clouds the issue about salvation and eternal life, they are more dangerous than thieves and murderers. They are vicious and ravenous dogs.

And in the phrase "mutilators of the flesh" we get a key to the error they were teaching. It had to do with the rite of circumcision. In fact, the Judaistic teachers in Paul's day sometimes called themselves "The Circumcision Party." They taught that Christ was the Messiah, and that He died to make it possible for believers to be saved. But they insisted that a person is saved only when he obeys all of the moral and ceremonial laws given to Israel—with special emphasis on circumcision.

Under the Law, a Jewish boy baby was taken to the synagogue when he was eight days old, and there the priest cut away the baby's foreskin. The custom had practical value in the realm of personal hygiene, but more important, it pictured the way God in Christ separates us from our condemned sinful nature (see Col. 2:11). The main value lay in the symbolism.

These "dogs" Paul writes about thought of circumcision as a necessary church sacrament. They taught that an uncircumcised man could not be admitted into heaven. To them the "gospel" was Christ's work plus man's obedience to all the rules and regulations. Paul considered their false doctrines a grave threat to the believer's spiritual welfare (see Gal. 5:2-4). He insisted that circumcision had nothing to do with a person's salvation. And he's ready to back that up with solid Old Testament verses.

So Paul refuses to dignify the false teachers by using the term, "Circumcision Party." He uses another word with a similar meaning. He calls them "mutilators."

Who Is "The Circumcision"?

Who, then, can rightly call himself, "The Circumcision"? The answer is given in three statements, and each statement is a step toward a clearer understanding of what it means to be a Christian.

1. We worship God by His Spirit, not by creating a religious climate or providing ourselves with worship tools.

2. We glory in Christ Jesus. We do not give ourselves points on our church affiliation, our personal discipline or our moral achievement.

3. We put no confidence in ourselves. We never get good enough or spiritual enough to merit our acceptance with God. He receives us by His grace.

Let's dig a little deeper into those three ideas in Paul's definition of a Christian.

We Worship God by His Spirit

What does it take to give you a worship experience? A picture of Jesus? Stained glass windows? Smoking incense? Some people don't feel comfortable in church unless the decorations or the rituals are what they're used to. Some people don't feel comfortable in church at all. For them, worship comes easier at the beach, on a hilltop.

A former hard-drinking sportswriter for the *Detroit News* got concerned a couple of years ago about the way Sunday schedules kept major league baseball players from going to church. "Waddy" Spoelstra's byline for years had kept Detroit baseball fans informed on the fortunes of the Tigers. Booze threatened his career until Waddy received Christ as Saviour and got a new set of priorities. That's when he began to worry about the spiritual plight of the players.

Getting baseball commissioner Bowie Kuhn's personal endorsement of his plan, Spoelstra took early retirement from the *News* and hit the road to organize a worship program for the superstars.

Now Reggie Jackson, Manny Sanguillen, Johnny Bench, Yogi Berra, Phil Regan and scores of other players, coaches and managers get together for chapel services before Sunday games. They meet in motel rooms, hotel lobbies, dining halls—even in locker rooms—to "worship God by His Spirit." There's no altar, no choir, no pulpit and no religious paraphernalia.

Rarely does an ordained minister speak at Baseball Chapel. Everything is informal. The message is usually brought by an athlete with recognized commitment to Christ, like Bobby Richardson and Alvin Dark. The only thing required for a real corporate worship experience is Christian people to participate, someone to minister God's Word and the presence of the Holy Spirit. When the first two factors are there, you can be sure that the Holy Spirit is there too.

We Glory in Christ Jesus

As a believer in Christ, what gives you your kicks? What's the purpose of your life? Christians can become proud of their church, proud of their good behavior, proud of their spirituality and proud that they associate with people they're proud of. On the other hand, some believers have found it is not a good idea to be proud of anything (see Prov. 29:23). They are just grateful and glad that Jesus accepts them and includes them in His eternal program. They "glory" only in knowing Him.

"Whenever we find that our religious life is making us feel we are better than someone else, we may be sure that we are being acted on, not by God, but by the devil," C.S. Lewis wrote in *Mere Christianity*.[1]

We Put No Confidence in Ourselves

What is the basis for your acceptance with God? Are you sure of your salvation because your character is improving? Do you feel accepted by God because you are superior to people who still indulge in worldly vices?

The most revolutionary truth is that God's acceptance of humans is not based on qualifications met by our "flesh." We are not capable of the kind of virtue or spirituality that would be needed to exempt us from God's judgment against all sin (see Rom. 7:18). God's goal for man is not that man improve so his body and mind become pure enough and disciplined enough to commend him to God. Man's goal is to recognize that works of merit and character development cannot save him (see Titus 3:5). There is no place for confidence in his own righteousness. Men get to God only by accepting His forgiveness in faith. And that forgiveness is offered only on the basis of Christ's substitutionary death for our sins.

True character development begins *after* a person has found a right relationship with God.

Good Works Aren't Enough

Paul could throw himself enthusiastically into a doctrine like that. As a religious zealot he knew the subtle dangers of spiritual self-satisfaction. He knew all about the human tendency to depend on our own religious accomplishments to get us to God. "I myself have reasons for such confidence," he closed the passage we read a few pages back. Now we're ready for a look at the qualifications Paul had once thought could earn him a place in God's Kingdom.

If anyone else thinks he has reasons to put confidence in the flesh, I have more: circumcised on the eighth day, of the people of Israel, of the tribe of Benjamin, a Hebrew of Hebrews; in regard to the law, a Pharisee; as for zeal, persecuting the church; as for legalistic righteousness, faultless (Phil. 3:4-6, *NIV*).

Unless we probe into them more deeply, those qualifications may seem things only a Jew could talk about. How would we apply circumcision, the tribe of Benjamin, the law and the Pharisees to the life we live today? The fact is, each of the points Paul makes as he describes his experiences lifts the lid of some possibility for error in our own point of view about God.

"If anyone else thinks he has reasons to put confidence in the flesh, I have more," he writes. It wouldn't impress us much to hear a lecture on the futility of good works from someone notoriously bad. We'd respond with a charge of "sour grapes"! The person who has never known anything but poverty is not the one to convince us riches breed unhappiness. We'd accept that idea more readily from a rich man who'd given his wealth away to find happiness.

Paul tried the "good works" approach and saw it fail. Therefore he's a man we can afford to listen to. Let's make a list of the factors he felt would close the

91

gap between himself and God—before he learned a better way.

1. *He'd been circumcised when he was eight days old, precisely as the law required.* Had Paul been an Ishmaelite, he'd have been circumcised as Ishmael was at the age of 13. Had he been a proselyte to the faith, the job would have been done at whatever age he joined the Jewish community. The magic words "eight days" speak of proper obedience to the exact letter of the law on the part of devout Jewish parents.

But many of us aren't Jews. Besides that, half of our readers are girls—who just can't work up a sense of involvement in matters pertaining to circumcision. Anyway, in most cases American boy babies are circumcised before they're eight *minutes* old. So what's the connection between circumcision and what's happening in our own lives near the end of the twentieth century?

The application is easier than you might think. That Jewish rite would symbolize today any religious obligation fulfilled on our behalf by someone else. Were you dedicated by Christian parents when you were a baby? Were certain prayers said for you, candles burned for you, signs made over your head?

If so, great! But these things move you no closer to God. They don't make you spiritual. They don't alter your status as a sinner in need of forgiveness.

2. *Paul was an Israelite, a product of the tribe of Benjamin, and in every respect a pure Hebrew.* Both of his parents were descendants of Jacob. Their tribe had given Israel its first king, the headstrong Saul. Within Benjamin's boundaries stood Jerusalem. Paul had been trained in the Holy City under the great

teacher, Gamaliel. He spoke fluent Hebrew and studied the Scriptures in the sacred language. Can you imagine someone with qualifications like that failing to make it to heaven?

But God doesn't play favorites, right? (see Acts 10:34). Therefore it wouldn't be biblical to think that the chance circumstances of birth and family tree could influence God's attitude toward any human being. Yet some very religious people act as if they think they do.

What about the guy who feels he's right with God because his grandfather and two uncles were ministers? Or because his parents were charter members of the city's best known church? Or because his sister sings in the choir?

A missionary to the Orient once asked an American soldier overseas if he was a Christian, to which the GI replied, "Why sure! Do I look like a Buddhist or something?"

I've known people who felt they had some sort of spiritual qualification because they happened to come from the "Bible Belt"—as if God is impressed by a southern accent!

3. *Paul was a member in good standing of a group called "Pharisees."* He belonged to the "just right" denomination. And it's not hard finding counterparts in "dyed-in-the-wool" church members today. I was raised in Southern Presbyterian, and until I became a Christian I was pretty sure God was a Southern Presbyterian too!

No church has a copyright on the truth or a patent on God. "Belonging" to a group doesn't prove anything about the real person down inside. Being classified a Pharisee had nothing to do with Paul's acceptance by God.

4. *No one surpassed Paul in religious zeal*. Before his own conversion he considered Christians dangerously misled people who threatened humanity with their heresy. He spent more time than any other Jewish official persecuting the church (see Gal. 1:13, 14). He really worked at it, in utter sincerity, believing himself to be God's instrument (see Acts 8:3; 9:1; 26:4,5,9-11).

Paul was trying to serve God, but he was misguided like the person who classifies himself an "active church member" but has never become personally acquainted with Jesus Christ!

5. *No one surpassed Paul in legalistic righteousness*. He was like the rich young ruler who told Jesus he had kept God's law since he was a boy (see Mark 10:20). Paul knew God's requirements for personal purity, and disciplined himself sternly to live by them.

The fact is, until the "Damascus Road" experience that changed his life (see Acts 9:1-6), Saul of Tarsus felt he turned in a pretty good performance for God. He was proud of his sinlessness.

What about someone who assumes he's right with God because he is "a good moral man"? Isn't he in the same category as the religious-but-lost person Paul discovered himself to be?

No matter how hard we try, or how much personal discipline we put into it, humans simply can't work up the kind of righteousness God requires (see Isa. 64:6). Therefore we cannot be saved by of our personal good behavior (see Eph. 2:8,9). We are saved when we realize our *bad* behavior has been covered by Christ. We are accepted because God's sinless Son traded places with us and died for our sins.

It's not good guys who get to heaven. It's bad guys who face up to their wrongness and accept the forgiveness God offers through Jesus Christ.

When we accept that forgiveness, God accepts us. Then we find out what happiness really is.

PUT IT TO WORK
1. Isn't this a good time to give some serious consideration to your own personal relationship with God? If you feel He has accepted you, on what do you base that opinion? Good theology isn't written on our feelings; it is found on the pages of God's Word.
2. Using whatever study tools you prefer, see how many Bible verses you can find that teach the doctrine of salvation-through-faith-not-works. You can get help on that assignment from your pastor, youth leader, Sunday School teacher or anyone else you feel may know the Word of God.
3. What would you look for if someone asked you to try to identify a "false teacher"? What might be the main point on which he differs from what the Bible teaches?

Footnote

1. C.S. Lewis, *Mere Christianity* (New York: The Macmillan Co., 1960), p. 111.

8

Philippians 3:7-16

DON'T LOOK BACK— SOMEONE'S GAINING

In the summer of 1975 newspapers carried the story of Gregorio Gorriz who was only 41 years old when he gained immortality at Pamplona's "running of the bulls." Unfortunately for Gregorio, he never got any older.

But Pamplonans will remember the bricklayer for years to come. They will, it is to be hoped, mention his name with the reverence due the fiftieth man gored to death in Spain's annual festival of drinking and derring-do. No one can deny that Gregorio has earned his place in history.

It is possible, however, he was not concerned with such details at the moment an enraged bull drove a horn through his chest.

The violent event at Pamplona is the highlight of a 400-year-old religious festival observed annually in

June in honor of San Fermin, patron saint of the city.

The bulls that participate are doomed to die by matadors' swords in Pamplona's Plaza de Toros. But before that event they stampede the half mile from the corral to the bull ring. Nearly 1500 brave men scamper before them, letting the bulls get so close they can feel their hot moist breath before darting out of reach.

Gregorio's mistake was looking back. He and scores of other runners failed to notice how small the gate was that led into the bull ring. By the time they looked ahead, it was too late. A dozen tried to get through the tiny opening at once, blocking the entrance. Several stumbled, and the pileup began. Gregorio tried to climb the fence, but fell to the ground in terror as crazed bulls charged into the mass of human bodies.

Several other men were injured—some painfully and a few gravely. But Gorriz alone had the distinction of a mortal wound. By the time the police got him to Pamplona's hospital, the unfortunate bricklayer was dead.

They will not soon forget you at Pamplona, Gregorio. They will sing of your bravery in the taverns of Barcelona and Madrid. But next time, look ahead. Keep your eye on the bull ring and not on the bull.

Concentrate on what's coming up, not what's gone before.

Don't Look Back
Paul practiced that "don't look back" philosophy. It comes through loud and clear in several verses of chapter 3.

There's a two-pronged danger in living in the past. The more obvious threat comes from dwelling on past mistakes and failures. The book of Philippians puts a lot of emphasis on that. But it also warns against depending on past honors and accomplishments.

It's self-defeating to look back and say, "I blew it—I'm no good!" But it's also bad news when we look back and say, "Man, I was really great that time! What a performance! Looks like I've got what it takes with plenty to spare!"

Paul goes into both of those dangers—though in reverse order. In the previous verses he recited his religious accomplishments and spiritual qualifications. Now we find him facing a solemn fact that everyone ought to face in sizing up his own relationship with God.

> But whatever was to my profit I now consider loss for the sake of Christ. What is more, I consider everything a loss compared to the surpassing greatness of knowing Christ Jesus my Lord, for whose sake I have lost all things. I consider them rubbish, that I may gain Christ and be found in him, not having a righteousness of my own that comes from the law, but that which is through faith in Christ —the righteousness that comes from God and is by faith. I want to know Christ and the power of his resurrection and the fellowship of sharing in his sufferings, becoming like him in his death, and so, somehow, to attain to the resurrection from the dead (Phil. 3:7-11, NIV).

There's a unique system of bookkeeping in those verses. It's not about dollars and cents, but it *is* about values. Paul's ledger began with some important entries in the beginning of chapter 3.

Remember?

On the asset side, he listed all the religious qualifications he had counted on before his dramatic conversion to Jesus Christ. You name it, he had it. History, geography, politics, prestige, background and foreground—everything was there in the proper column to classify Paul as a man who took God seriously. His was no halfhearted commitment. His behavior—or at least the visible part of it—was flawless. He kept all the rules and regulations and met all the requirements—at least as far as anyone knew. Jews in every direction could point to him with pride and say, "God really hit the jackpot when he got Saul of Tarsus on His side!"

What Really Counts

But that kind of thinking jars a little if you consider the stark realities of life. Did this man have something the rest of us missed? Were we passed over when they handed out perfection to human beings? We don't have the ability to turn in a flawless performance, and we know it. Sure, we're sincere, and we always have the best of intentions, but we've fallen flat too often to hold any illusions about perfection being part of our bag.

But Saul of Tarsus thought it was, and he worked long and hard to attain it. The time came, though, when he gave it up as a bummer. That's when Saul became Paul. That's when law gave way to grace. He had failed to reckon with God's definition of perfection. Saul figured 8 or 9 on a scale of 10 would get him through the pearly gates. But God's holy requirements allow no demerits at all!

The person who hopes to get to heaven by being good has to be as good as God from the moment he is born until the moment he dies! Are you acquainted with even a single human being who could meet a standard like that? (See Rom. 3:23.)

Donny's testimony came through something like Paul's when he shared his experience with other teenagers on the final night of youth camp. Thinking about it the first time, he wasn't sure he'd be able to say exactly what he wanted to say—his back to the roaring campfire and a hundred or so campers trying to relate his feelings to their own. But he took a deep breath and got to his feet, and it seemed God sort of took over from there.

Donny's parents were Christians and he'd been raised to tell the truth, go to Sunday School, read his Bible, pray, say the blessing before meals, be honest about money, be careful of his language and be careful about girls. He'd been dedicated and baptized and had joined the church on Easter Sunday morning when he was 12.

But while things were in pretty good shape on the outside, Donny had realized for a couple of years things weren't what they ought to be on the inside, and that bothered him. He was religious, but he'd begun to wonder if a guy could be religious and lost at the same time. According to Paul, a guy certainly can!

Things began to make sense for Donny the second

morning of camp after Mack Stanford got into his Bible study series on Titus 3:5. A whole week of Bible studies on just one verse of Scripture! By the second morning, the pieces were fitting together. By Friday, everything was clear. God doesn't save a person because of his clean habits, good living and church activities. It's an act of His mercy—something that couldn't have happened without the special sacrifice Jesus made for us. Salvation can't be earned. It has to be accepted by faith as a gift that can never be deserved.

Profit or Loss?

When Saul became Paul, he had to make a radical change in his bookkeeping system. The things he figured as assets suddenly became liabilities. What seemed profit to Saul became loss to Paul. That's because Paul began to see things the way God sees them. He began to draw his ideas from the Word of God instead of from the religious system and opinions that surrounded him.

That's the point of view from which he wrote, "I know that nothing good lives in me, that is, in my sinful nature. For I have the desire to do what is good, but I cannot carry it out. For what I do is not the good I want to do; no, the evil I do not want to do—this I keep on doing" (Rom. 7:18,19, *NIV*).

Does that sound like the man who prided himself on his religiosity and personal purity? The change came when he realized that God is infinitely greater than we are. He is incapable of any human imperfection (see Ps. 92:15). His concepts of rightness and justice go far beyond anything mere mortals are capable of grasping. So trying to impress God or gain His approval by our good behavior is like trying to get the attention of the world's richest person by waving a two-dollar bill in his face.

"Once I thought everything depended on what I could do for God," Paul says in the verses we read a short while ago. "Now I realize it depends on what God has done for me. My performance counts for nothing—zero—nowheresville. It's garbage. What matters is a personal acquaintance with Jesus Christ. Knowing Him beats anything else religion has to offer—or demand."

Then he reveals the secret that eluded him for all those years as a hard-working Pharisee. It's a pivotal truth that goes on eluding religious people through the centuries until they learn what Christ's ministry is all about. Righteousness could only come through unfailing obedience to the laws of God. But man is not capable of that kind of performance. So he needs to obtain a righteousness in God's sight through some other means. This righteousness comes not from man's limited resources, but from God Himself. It comes through the channel of our faith, and that faith begins to function when we settle in on a fact that seems incredible. God will accept us on the basis of the flawless performance of His Son. Jesus lived the kind of life we ought to live, and He died the death we would have to die because we haven't measured up. That's His gift of love to us.

How do you respond when you hear the good news about Christ's death for our sins? To believe it—really do business with it as a settled truth—required a concept of God's greatness, goodness and grace you never understood before. It demands a shift away from that backward, inward look that focuses on your supposed merits. It says, "Look to God's Son, and accept the fact that He obeyed God's laws *for* you, in *your place*, then died for your sins."

That's where identification with Christ begins. From that point on, God's grace takes the believer to a growing experience of power stemming from Christ's resurrection.

In this life with Christ there's no looking inward or backward on proud achievements that presumably commend us to God. We look outward to the perfect performance of Jesus as our representative. And we look forward to the deepening, growing relationship with Christ we can enjoy because He accepts us without question or demands. We don't even protest the suffering we may experience. It builds character. It gives us a "resurrection" of sorts from the deadly danger of our own ego trips.

But even suffering does not make us perfect. "I do not know what I am doing. For what I want to do I do not do, but what I hate I do," Paul testifies concerning his struggle to get rid of his sins (Rom. 7:15, *NIV*). We aspire to live as God would have us, and with all our hearts we wish that could be the case here and now. But experience and observation convince us failure will haunt us, even at the pinnacle of spiritual achievement. We will never be able to boast, "Look at me, everybody—I've arrived. I've finally become the spiritual giant I knew I'd be some day."

No One's Perfect Yet

"Not me," says Paul. He was head and shoulders

above most of us, but he knew he had more growing to do. Here is the way he states the case.

> *Not that I have already obtained all this, or have already been made perfect, but I press on to take hold of that for which Christ Jesus took hold of me. Brothers, I do not consider myself yet to have taken hold of it. But one thing I do: Forgetting what is behind and straining toward what is ahead, I press on toward the goal to win the prize for which God has called me heavenward in Christ Jesus* (Phil. 3:12-14, *NIV*).

Paul had a proven formula he was eager to share with the Christians at Philippi—and with all of us today. He refused to look back, either to presume on his successes or to lament his failures. He handled the past with a three-syllable vocabulary: "Forget it!"

Learning from our mistakes is one thing; brooding over them and carrying their weight on our backs is another.

A 25-year-old Kansas City golf pro named Tom Watson (sorry, no kin!) held a comfortable lead in the early rounds of successive U.S. Open tournaments in 1974 and 1975. He tensed up, though, as the going got tough and blew it under pressure both years with highly unprofessional rounds of 79.

Tom was interviewed on national television after the 1975 debacle at Medinah and asked if he was disgusted with himself for coming apart at the seams with victory almost in his grasp. He said he wasn't mad—not at himself or anyone else.

"I don't think it hurts us to fail," he told the TV audience, "providing we learn from our mistakes. I'm going to concentrate on improving my game, and maybe I'll play better in the next tournament I enter."

He managed to do just that. Only a month later at Carnoustie, Scotland, he finished ahead of veterans like Jack Nicklaus, Hale Irwin, Tom Weiskopf and Johnny Miller to meet Australian Jack Newton in an 18-hole playoff for the British Open championship.

It was pressure all the way, with first one player a stroke under and then the other. They were tied at one under par going into the eighteenth hole for a cliff-hanging finish.

Watson was steady as a surgeon's scalpel, while Newton's drive nestled in a bunker near the green. That cost the Australian a stroke—the single shot that proved Tom Watson's margin of victory.

"I made a slight change in my swing," the winner explained. He had looked back, but only to profit by his mistakes.

"Don't look back, somebody might be gaining on you," is a remark often attributed to Jackie Robinson, one of baseball's all-time greats. It might be the specter of guilt or fear, with an insistent reminder about things better off forgotten.

Lot's wife looked back, and became a pillar of salt (see Gen. 19:26). Sodom and Gomorrah represented failures that merited the judgment of God. Lot's wife should have fixed her eyes on Zoar, God's appointed city of refuge. Instead, she found fatal attraction in the brimstone and fire falling behind her. In the moment she stole that backward glance, she lost everything. What was real and important lay ahead. What lay behind her should have been buried in the sea of

God's forgetfulness and never remembered again.

Concentrate on the Goal

"I haven't won any prizes yet," Paul writes. "I'm a long way from the legitimate goal of perfection. I've still got lots to learn. So I'm concentrating on the goal that's out there ahead of me. If I look back, it will only serve to frighten or discourage me. Everything I'm living for is out there ahead—all the things Christ had in mind for me when He gave me a part in His program. I'm happy to leave it all under His control."

That gives the initiative back to the Son of God. We can take hold of Him because He took hold of us. We can reach out in faith for what He offers as He reaches out in mercy to us.

Hank and Joan found that truth vital and real as they settled down to the job of making a home for their baby daughter, Jill. Jill was a baby who really wasn't supposed to be. Hank and Joan had just finished high school when Joan learned she was pregnant—by Hank, of course. The two kids weren't married, but they were in love. So after some long and painful sessions with their pastor and two sets of embarrassed and heart-broken parents they all agreed a wedding was the only acceptable solution to a bad situation.

"You both are guilty of a very serious offense in God's sight," their wise pastor told them. "And that's something you've got to make right with Him. But you've asked for God's forgiveness, for your parents' forgiveness and you've asked for mine, and as far as I'm concerned the sin has been dealt with and disposed of. Now the important thing is to deal properly with the consequence of your sin. I'd suggest that both of you forgive yourselves and get on with the business of establishing a Christian home and family for the glory of God. Just settle it right now that what's past is past—okay?"

From that moment on, neither the pastor nor their parents ever mentioned their failure again.

You'll never find a Christian who hasn't met with some form of failure or disappointment during his experience as a believer. Some of us make worse mistakes—or more frequent blunders—than others, but no one can boast a flawless performance. Enough of our humanity still is with us to louse up the record.

Discouragement is the most effective weapon in the devil's arsenal. It tears at our vitals, disarms us, weakens our resistance and makes us sitting ducks for the first shotgun blast of doubt to sweep across our position.

The language Paul uses is drawn from the Greek athletic arena, where contenders strained their muscles and lungs to the breaking point. Nothing was important to them except the finish line ahead. "Let us throw off everything that hinders and the sin that so easily entangles, and let us run with perseverance the race marked out for us," the writer of Hebrews expressed it (Heb. 12:1, *NIV*). Energy and time wasted in looking back, pouting and brooding over past mistakes, might well cost us the victory.

The real tragedy in the backward look is not just the lost momentum and the blurred goal. It's the futility of it all. Nothing can be gained by dwelling on past sins. The script can never be rewritten. The damage can never be undone.

Undone, no; repaired, yes. Nothing Paul says here excuses the Christian from making things right when his mistakes cause hurt or loss to others. It's not "looking back" to pay for the damages. No one ever turned to salt because he acknowledged his errors and asked for forgiveness. That's simple obedience to the command of God (see Matt. 5:23,24).

In spite of a lot of advantages other kids didn't have, Rod managed to foul up his life completely before he finished the tenth grade. His Christian parents suffered heartache and despair for four full years as they watched him grow more defiant and less responsible for his childish acts of rebellion. By the time he was 18 it looked as though he was hopelessly committed to a life centered around narcotics, booze, women, odd jobs and conflict with the police. He was angry with his family and his family was angry with him, so Rod moved out and found a place of his own.

But though his parents gave up pleading and fighting back, they never gave up praying and trusting God for specific answers. And the day came when Rod rang their doorbell, told of his newly discovered faith in Christ, and asked to be forgiven.

Then began the long road back to a life of purpose and meaning. Rod had a keen mind, and he managed to pass the exam for a Graduate Equivalency Diploma. This opened up job opportunities and a chance to enroll in the local junior college. Within a year after his conversion to Christ he was down the road toward a career as a surgical technician.

Rod had made some painful and costly mistakes, but he didn't brood over them. He didn't waste time feeling sorry for himself. He didn't consider himself a dropout from the human race, and his parents didn't make him feel like one. And Rod didn't panic on the rare occasions when someone insisted on dredging up those old failures.

"They were bad mistakes, and I'm to blame for them," Rod once said to his father. "But I'm not going to spend the rest of my life with my tail between my legs. God has forgiven me, and you and Mom have forgiven me, and I guess that's all I need to go on from here.

"I've put it all behind me, and that's where it's going to stay. All I want to do now is look ahead to some of the good things I've got planned for the future with the help of a mighty understanding Lord."

So don't look back. Someone really might be gaining on you. And it's going to take your total concentration to reach the goal up ahead.

How's Your Growth Chart?

It's been well over 20 years since Roger Bannister became the first man on record to run a mile in less than four minutes.

Until May 6, 1954, four minutes was like a sound barrier to the mile run. It seemed physically impossible for a man to run that far that fast. In fact, it took something like 72 years for milers to shave 20 seconds off Walter George's time of 4:19.4. George chalked up that record on June 3, 1882.

But little by little, track meet by track meet, the time goes on shrinking. In the summer of 1975 a tall, rugged New Zealander named John Walker ran the mile in 3:49.4 at the Goteborg Games in Sweden.

That's exactly 10 seconds faster than Bannister's time, and a full half minute better than the 1882 record.

Figure it this way: for more than 80 years the world's runners have improved the mile record by something like 36-hundredths of a second per year. If that rate continues, we'll have a three and three-quarter-minute mile by 1988. But don't depend on that rule. If you kept on extending that graph you'd have someone running a mile in two minutes flat by the year 2305. And after that . . . ?

We can't improve a track record to the point of absurdity. But for a Christian, improvement is as much a part of life as salvation and going to heaven. Being a Christian doesn't mean you've arrived at your destination; it means you're on the way. You're learning and growing. Sometimes your progress may seem a lot less than 36-hundredths of a second per year. But by the grace of God, you're getting there. And you can get all the help and encouragement you need from the Lord Himself.

That doesn't mean that you'll be able to measure your spiritual growth on a nice, steady upward grade like this:

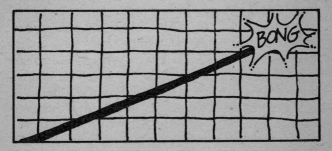

That's not a true-to-life pattern of growth. If you're honest with yourself (and what's the sense in being otherwise?) your chart will look more like this:

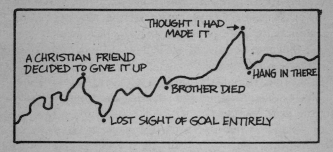

THOUGHT I HAD MADE IT →

A CHRISTIAN FRIEND DECIDED TO GIVE IT UP

HANG IN THERE

BROTHER DIED

LOST SIGHT OF GOAL ENTIRELY

"Straining toward what is ahead" is the way Paul describes his own experience. He doesn't boast about past accomplishments or weep over past failures. There's something out ahead that's worth all the effort, the pain, the heartache and the agony of occasional failure.

Christopher Columbus had that attitude when he sailed westward "to the Orient" from Spain, convinced that Japan lay 3000 miles across the Atlantic. Three weeks out of the Canary Islands—longer than ships had ever sailed before without a glimpse of land—his men began to fear they'd never see home and loved ones again. They were near mutiny. But Columbus persuaded them to sail only three more days before turning back. Two days later, Columbus sighted an island in the Bahamas which he named San Salvador. He had, in fact, "discovered America."

Had they turned back earlier, would America ever have been found? You better believe it! It was there. Other explorers would have persevered sooner or later. But it was Christopher Columbus who "strained toward what was ahead." In spite of discouragement at home, storms, mutiny at sea and unknown hardships beyond the western horizon, he stayed on course. So it was Columbus who got the prize from King Ferdinand and Queen Isabella.

Christian Maturity

All of us who are mature should take such a view of things. And if on some point you think differently, that too God will make clear to you. Only let us live up to what we have already attained (Phil. 3:15,16, *NIV*).

Paul says the mature Christian will share his view of life as described in verses 13 and 14. What does he mean by "mature"? Spiritual maturity involves an understanding of God's process of character development. Saying "I'm a Christian" is not a claim to be better than anyone else. To say that I'm a believer in Christ does not mean I feel I've reached a plateau of sinless perfection. It means I've faced up to the harsh realities of life. I know that I'm not what I ought to be, and that God imposes a harsh penalty for my sins. He says I have to die.

If that weren't the case, there wouldn't be any need for the gospel of Christ. God's Son died so the penalty for my faults and failures could be paid in full. That way God is able to forgive the goofs of yesterday, today and tomorrow—and keep on forgiving— because that way He can maintain the moral balance of His universe.

That means being a Christian is not a contest to see if I can hold out and not do anything really bad—or at least not get caught at it. It's a matter of doing my best and admitting it when I'm wrong. It's profiting from my mistakes and thanking God for my progress. It's believing that out there in the distance there's a "prize" waiting for all of us when we finish the course. That's right, *all* of us who rest our case in the dependable hands of Jesus Christ. He won't discard any of us as unworthy. If worthiness had anything to do with it, we'd all end up in hell.

"Forgetting what is behind and straining toward what is ahead" is the most workable attitude for any of us, whether we're young or old, weak or strong. Paul insists that this is the spiritually mature point of view. And he writes further that if anyone fails to see it that way . . .well, he'll come around to the right way of thinking in due time. God will "reveal" it. Right now he's simply not able to grasp the facts. In God's good time, he will.

We have common cause, though, with people who recognize that spiritual growth involves failures as well as successes. Working side by side with people like that, we can understand each other. We can forgive, because God forgives (see Eph. 4:32). We accept others because He accepts us. Our theme still is "my utmost for His highest" (see Phil. 1:20), but we've learned not to expect the impossible—not from ourselves and not from others.

Kim saw it that way when she suggested a "forgive and forget" society in her church in central Kansas. She suggested that all the kids who were holding a grudge against anybody meet one night a month and without mentioning any names or disclosing any embarrassing circumstances share with each other the things that were bugging them about the person.

In many cases the kids admitted their grudges were childish and ridiculous at the same time they unloaded their feelings. In almost every case, reconciliation took place soon after the facts were flushed out into the open.

"Nobody's perfect—not even me," Kim said with a twinkle in her eye. "As soon as we began to really believe that, we found we could accept each other better and understand the way God accepts us in spite of our sin."

PUT IT TO WORK

1. Check out a few assorted contemporary translations of the New Testament and choose the version of Philippians 3:12-14 that makes the most sense to you. Then take the time to memorize these three short verses and make them a part of your own defense against discouragement.

2. What are some of the situations in which you are most tempted to look back? Can you reduce this threat by preparing yourself right now against these situations? Think up a practical and workable way you can handle this temptation and be ready to use your defense weapons the moment you realize you're in danger again.

3. Are you having trouble handling past mistakes because you've been afraid or unwilling to make things right with someone you hurt? Decide right now on a time and a way to get that important job taken care of so you can give your full attention to the goal that lies ahead.

4. Your assignment: think back over your life as a Christian and decide how you'd show your spiritual growth on a graph. Has it zoomed? Gone in spurts? Hit rock bottom?

Make your graph cover from there to here in terms of years. Maybe a scale of 1 to 10—or 1 to 100—would do to show your spirituality improving.

Now draw your graph line. Start at the beginning, when you first became a Christian. Put notations beside the high and low points to explain what was happening then.

File your graph for future reference.

9

WE'LL BE
DIFFERENT
SOMEDAY

Have you ever watched a little boy pretending to drive a car "just like daddy"? Or a little girl trying on her mother's high heels? Children learn early to follow their parents' example.

Later on, when we get a little older, we look around for somebody else to imitate. Sometimes we're not as careful as we should be in our choice. Other times we're fortunate enough to pick a good example and to profit by imitating that person.

A Good Example to Follow

Paul has a suggestion for the Philippian believers—and for you and me as well:

> Join with others in following my example, brothers, and take note of those who live according to the pattern we gave you (Phil. 3: 17, NIV).

Paul wasn't afraid to encourage the believers to follow his example. He just admitted he hadn't arrived, so we can't accuse him of having an inflated

116

ego. Rather, he realizes people learn by imitating others. Therefore he says, "If you're going to imitate someone, be careful whom you choose!" Paul not only points to himself as a good example to follow, but he also suggests, "take note of those who live according to the pattern we gave you."

Take a look around you. Do you see people who are living according to the principles laid down by Paul and others in Scripture? Don't be misled by superficial charm or a flashy gift of gab. Take a close look at a person's life before you decide to follow his or her example. Make sure a person's life measures up to the standard before you pattern yours after his.

Avoid the Bad Examples

Paul also includes a warning about some people who are definitely bad examples, not to be imitated by the Christian.

> For, as I have often told you before and now say again even with tears, many live as enemies of the cross of Christ. Their destiny is destruction, their god is their stomach, and their glory is in their shame. Their mind is on earthly things (Phil. 3:18,19, NIV).

Who are these enemies of the cross of Christ? Why does Paul speak so severely and sadly about them?

There are many people who teach things about God and man that aren't true. Their point of view comes from man's mind, not from God's Word. These may be people who live only for themselves and their own pleasure. Paul has a picturesque way of wording it—"their god is their stomach"—but the message is clear.

117

Others focus on "earthly" ways of earning God's favor. They teach that man's relationship with God is based on man's ability to please God by working hard. That kind of doctrine is based on human feelings, not divine facts (see Eph. 2:8,9). To teach that man can earn God's approval by being good, proving his sincerity, or keeping a set of rules, sends him down the well-paved path to destruction.

God doesn't save a person because he obeys a rule or observes a formula. That would give him room for boasting, and God won't allow that (see Eph. 2:9). Man in his natural sinful state is not just temporarily indisposed; he is dead (see Eph. 2:1). It takes an act of God's sovereign grace to make him live. Man is powerless to do it himself.

To teach that people have to do or avoid doing something to be saved is to place on them a burden heavier than they can bear. It's misleading them about God's way of salvation.

And what is God's way? The Bible warns that people are unable to save themselves, no matter how hard they try or how nearly perfect they consider themselves. It tells that God punishes all human imperfection—that no man is perfect (see Rom. 3:23; 1 John 1:8-10) and therefore all must be punished. But the Bible also says that Jesus died in our place and took the punishment for our sins (see Rom. 5:6-9; 1 Pet. 2:24; 3:18) so that whoever believes in Him can have eternal life (see John 3:16; Rom. 10:9,10). The Bible urges people to believe that fact and accept by faith the relationship God offers through Christ (see Rom. 6:23).

Furthermore, we can trust on the authority of His

Word that God will see to it that Christians grow. Mistakes will happen. Disappointments and setbacks will come. But Christ's substitutionary death also paid the price for those sins. And in spite of the pain and strain of our mistakes, we move on toward spiritual maturity (see Phil. 1:6; 2:13).

The forgiveness and unconditional acceptance God offers us in Christ can't be purchased or earned (see Titus 3:5,6). God says that we must simply step forward through faith in Christ and receive the undeserved blessings He is pleased to give us (see Eph. 2:8; Rom. 10:9,10). No strings are attached. The person who adds conditions to God's free offer is neither God's friend nor ours.

But it is understandable that the idea of unconditional acceptance causes some sincere Christians genuine concern. After all, plenty of verses in the Bible such as 1 John 3:9 and John 14:15 equate Christianity with righteous living. Romans 13:13 says every believer should be an honest, upright person. The entire Sermon on the Mount in Matthew 5 through 7 is designed to motivate us to live the way God desires.

It's hard to believe a person really belongs to Jesus Christ if he justifies his bad behavior by claiming God doesn't really mind. God does mind, and that concern is voiced in many verses urging His people to be good (see Matt. 5:48).

Yet nowhere does God threaten to throw us out when we fall short of His ideal. He knows we'll chalk up a few failures. He knows exactly what to expect of us and what not to expect. And patiently He teaches us what we need to know in order to grow, no matter how slow or painful the lessons prove to be. In theological terms, that process is called "sanctification." And it's guaranteed to get the desired results.

The end result of sanctification is a righteousness patterned after God's own character (see Rom. 8:29). It is a settled fact with God that every believer will become the intended finished product. But the process is not complete until we stand in the presence of God in eternity (see 1 John 3:2).

We've seen how the "enemies of the cross" were enemies because their doctrine came from man, not God. Another aspect of their error had to do with their values. "Their mind is on earthly things." They saw things only from an earthly point of view. Everything began and ended in this life. This thinking can lead to serious distortions in one's way of looking at things, since our lives do *not* end with the end of earthly life. The human personality survives the grave—and its ultimate destination, for good or for bad, depends on the decisions made while on earth.

Citizens of Heaven

Paul contrasts the "earthly minded" people to the Christians:

> But our citizenship is in heaven. And we eagerly await a Savior from there, the Lord Jesus Christ, who, by the power that enables him to bring everything under his control, will transform our lowly bodies so that they will be like his glorious body (Phil. 3:20,21, NIV).

Paul says a Christian is a citizen of heaven. We're not living in heaven yet, but that's where we belong.

In this world we are more like visitors in a foreign country (see 1 Pet. 1:11).

As citizens of heaven, our privileges are great. We have been born into the family of God. God is our heavenly Father; Jesus Christ is our Redeemer; the Holy Spirit is our Comforter and Teacher. We can come directly to God in prayer for ourselves and others. We can receive forgiveness and cleansing for our sins. We have God's guidance and protection. Satan can't bring any charge against us, because Christ will step in and say, "I've already taken care of this on the cross." We belong to God; we're citizens of His Kingdom.

But our citizenship involves some responsibilities too. A citizen of heaven ought to follow heaven's rules and laws, as well as the rules and laws of the place where he lives.

When a person born in another country decides he wants to become a citizen of the United States, he has to learn what it means to be a U.S. citizen. He studies U.S. history, the Constitution, and form of government. He has to meet certain residence requirements and have good moral character. When he can meet the requirements and demonstrate his knowledge of the required material, he appears before a judge and is granted citizenship papers.

The procedure is a bit different with heavenly citizenship. You become a citizen *first*; then you enter into the process of learning how to *be* a citizen. It's a lifetime of learning, so it's a good thing the Lord doesn't make us pass the test and meet the requirements before He lets us into His Kingdom!

Once you're in God's Kingdom, you find yourself

learning and growing in unexpected ways. You'll probably find that you're becoming uncomfortable with your worldly friends. The more their standards differ from God's, the more uncomfortable you'll be. This might confuse you, until you understand that a citizen of heaven has different values and different viewpoints from the citizens of the world. You can't expect to be at ease with people who lie and cheat, who make fun of Christians and use the Lord's name in vain, who use illegal drugs, who enjoy pornographic literature and obscene stories.

Even if your worldly friends don't do anything really wrong, you'll find that your values are different from theirs and that your belief in God and His Word will make you different from them.

A high school senior received the Lord shortly before graduation. Her Christian friends encouraged her to read the Bible and other Christian literature, and so she began to grow. One day she came across a reference to the devil, and was very surprised to realize that she now believed he was real! That's the sort of thing that happens to a citizen of heaven.

Citizens of heaven find that they have more in common with one another than they do with worldly people. As you grow in Christ, your values become more like His, and therefore more like those of other Christians. You worship the same Lord. You read the same Bible. You learn day by day to care for one another as the Lord cares for you.

You won't become perfect overnight—or in 50 years. But your citizenship guarantees you the right to get up after you stumble and to keep on going.

Hope is something else we get as citizens of heaven. "We eagerly await a Saviour" who is coming again. Have you ever had your best friend go away for a vacation? Did you eagerly await his or her return? If so, you know something of what it is like to eagerly await the Saviour. He is the most wonderful person in the universe, and we *know* He is coming back to take us home with Him. That's a great hope!

And not only will we be with Him, we will be changed to be like Him. No more colds, no more pimples and warts, no more aches and pains and terrible diseases. No more sin! Our bodies will be like His "glorious body." Remember the way the disciples saw Jesus after His resurrection? That's the way He is now, and that's the way we shall be. If you have a handicap or a chronic illness, if you don't like the shape of your nose or the way you give in so easily to sin, take heart! The day is coming when all of that will be swept away by His mighty power in changing you to be like Himself.

And meanwhile, you can tune in to that power to make your life here entirely different. You may not lose your handicap or chronic illness here on earth, but God can use those things like a carpenter uses sandpaper on a piece of furniture—to get rid of the rough spots and make you a more beautiful person (see Rom. 5:3-5; Jas. 1:2-4). He can help you forget the shape of your nose because you're so caught up in loving and serving Him you have no time to fret about your looks. And as for the sin, He'll forgive and cleanse you, and teach you step by step to overcome (see 1 John 1:9; Phil. 2:13).

How can you find happiness? Follow Paul's example; don't get bogged down thinking only about this earth, but remember that you are a citizen of heaven. Learn day by day how to live up to your heavenly citizenship, and look forward eagerly to the coming of the Lord. Then you'll see life in the right perspective, and you'll be happy living here and looking forward to your new home and new body in heaven.

PUT IT TO WORK

1. Draw a picture frame to fit around the mirror you use each day. Label the frame "Citizen of Heaven" and attach it to your mirror. Every time you look at yourself, remember that you are a citizen of heaven.

2. As you read the Bible, keep a notebook on "The Life-Style of a Citizen of Heaven." When you read about the early disciples (in the book of Acts, for example) make notes of things they do that are worthy of a citizen of heaven. When you read teaching portions (like the epistles), keep track of things Christians are told to do (for example, "Rejoice in the Lord" from Phil. 3:1).

   Let your notebook grow as you study the Bible over a period of months. Look through it now and then and check yourself against your notes on the way a citizen of heaven should be living.

3. A special section of your notebook could be devoted to Paul. He said to follow his example, and you'll have to find out how he lived if you're to do that. Study his life in Acts. You'll also find hints in his various letters to the churches. Check it out and write it down. Then check to see how you're doing.

10

HOW TO FIND REAL PEACE OF MIND

Jody and Cindy had a problem. They were Christians who were active in their youth group at church. They had worked together in the group, serving the Lord and bringing His message to others. They were good friends, too—at least, they had been until the argument.

One day Jody and Cindy were helping to plan a social. They found themselves on opposite sides of a disagreement. Jody and several others thought that the youth pastor should give a message and an invitation at the end of the social. The others—including Cindy—thought that several of the young people should tell what Jesus means to them.

Somehow—and no one was sure just how it happened—the discussion became an argument and the argument became a fight between Jody and Cindy. Now they weren't even speaking to one another. You could feel the tension in the air whenever they were both in the room. The whole group was affected by their attitude. The newer Christians couldn't understand how such a thing could happen, and some of them were stumbling in their faith because of it. The older Christians were concerned about this and about the effect of the fight on the testimony of the whole group.

What a problem! What do you suppose the apostle Paul would say if he were to write a letter to this youth group?

Help Our Sisters

He might say something similar to what he said to the Philippian church about a problem they had.

> *Therefore, my brothers, you whom I love and long for, my joy and crown, that is how you should stand firm in the Lord, dear friends! I plead with Euodia and I plead with Syntyche to agree with each other in the Lord. Yes, and I ask you, loyal yokefellow, help these women who have contended at my side in the cause of the gospel, along with Clement and the rest of my fellow workers, whose names are in the book of life* (Phil. 4:1-3, NIV).

Notice Paul's gentle and loving attitude. He is pleading, not browbeating. He doesn't say, "Okay, you two, shape up! You're messing up the church, so snap out of it! " He doesn't put them down; he wants to lift them up.

126

Euodia and Syntyche—or we could call them Jody and Cindy—had a disagreement. Maybe, in the midst of the emotions that had been aroused, they forgot that all believers are part of the same Body, and therefore ought to be more concerned about each other's needs than each other's faults.

We don't know the exact nature of their problem—just that they disagreed. But the disagreement was important enough for news to travel all the way from Philippi to Paul's quarters in Rome. Probably Epaphroditus included it in the report he made when he joined Paul.

What would a Jody and a Cindy hassle about in your youth group today? How to decorate the youth group's meeting place? The "right" kind of music for a social? Jealousy over a guy? You don't have to overwork your imagination to think of other possibilities.

Why is it important anyway? Why should Paul want to insert himself into a private hassle between two Christians? Because everything that happens in the Body of Christ is important to the *whole* Body and to the people that the Body is supposed to be winning to Christ.

So Paul asks some of the other believers to help Jody and Cindy get together. And while he's at it he reminds them all that the two women have served Christ right alongside the apostle. He holds up before them a picture of their high calling as servants of Christ, in the hope that this will help them get a new perspective on their problem. When we look at things from the Lord's point of view we tend to see them differently. We realize that petty, personal conflicts can't be allowed to hinder the cause of Christ.

How to Handle a Hassle

Christianity is just as much a way of life as a way to heaven. The Bible gives us detailed instructions on handling personality conflicts, and insists that we learn to settle our differences like mature people.

"Therefore, if you are offering your gift at the altar and there remember that your brother has something against you, leave your gift there in front of the altar," Jesus instructs us in the Sermon on the Mount. "First go and be reconciled to your brother; then come and offer your gift" (Matt. 5:23,24, *NIV*).

That covers the case where you have fouled up some way and offended someone. Maybe his feelings are justified and maybe they aren't, but who's to blame is not the issue in God's sight. God is concerned that conflict has arisen between two of His people. Spiritual blessing is short-circuited. Good vibrations are gone until the opponents get together and iron out their difficulties. So you are told to take the initiative, make the first move and restore the relationship that got lost along the way.

The situation may even require that you say you're sorry and ask for forgiveness. You may have to lay aside your pride and confess that you were wrong. It goes against all your instincts, but you may have to admit that you handled things the wrong way, had the wrong attitude, said the wrong words, treated someone like you wouldn't want to be treated yourself.

Where do we get the idea that a person shrinks a little when he says "I'm wrong"? He doesn't get smaller; he grows. Saying "I'm sorry—forgive me" is not admitting you're little; it's proving you're big!

A Florida newspaper carried the account of some teenagers in Oviedo, Florida, who found it very hard to say, "I'm sorry." Two girls who rode the school bus got tired of the marijuana smoke that filled the bus each morning with no objection from the driver. They reported the matter to the local police chief, who happened to be a friend of one of their families.

Smoking grass is a misdemeanor in Florida, so the police chief cracked down. As a result, the two girls were ostracized by their classmates, threatened, and finally beaten up. The situation got so bad that their parents were forced to take them out of school. Things would have been a lot different if the law-breakers had been willing to say, "I'm sorry. You caught me in the act and I was wrong."

What bad relationship is bugging you right now—nudging your conscience about someone you've mistreated or offended? Is it up to you to take the first step toward reconciliation?

Then get moving. "First go and be reconciled to your brother." Other duties can wait. You're carrying a big handicap if you're trying to serve the Lord with bad feelings working against you. Never mind asking about the other guy's responsibilities in the matter. That's his problem. Your duty is to set the machinery in motion. The time to do it is right now.

And sometimes the shoe is on the other foot. The problem is not that you've offended someone; he's offended you. You caught him in the act. He had his chance and he blew it. You're disappointed in him—maybe a little embittered. You can't picture yourself

129

ever again feeling close to a guy who'd do a thing like that.

Does the Bible have a word about that kind of situation? Try this on for size.

"Brothers, if a man is trapped in some sin, you who are spiritual should restore him gently. But watch yourself; you also may be tempted. Carry each other's burdens, and in this way you will fulfill the law of Christ" (Gal. 6:1,2, *NIV*).

Restore—that's the key word. The object is to mend the differences and heal the wounds. The reason is that the Body of Christ needs the other guy as much as it needs me. The real war is not between the good guys (us, of course) and the people we disagree with, don't like or don't approve of. The battle is between all of us and the devil. We can't afford to have a fellow soldier on the disabled list any longer than absolutely necessary.

The Christian who goofs is not my enemy; he's a wounded soldier who needs my help. He's still my brother, my fellow worker and my companion in arms.

Remember Paul says, "For our struggle is not against flesh and blood, but against the rulers, against the authorities, against the powers of this dark world and against the spiritual forces of evil in the heavenly realms" (Eph. 6:12, *NIV*).

A lot of ground is lost to the enemy because Christians turn their weapons on each other. We shouldn't be fighting each other; we should be standing together to fight off the powers of darkness, the spiritual forces of evil. That's why the apostle pleads for harmony among the Christians at Philippi. There's a war going on—and Christians can't afford any fighting among themselves when they should be battling the real enemy.

How to Find Peace of Mind

Having gently and lovingly urged the church to settle its differences, Paul turns to a new and important topic: the way to find peace of mind and heart in the midst of this world with all its hassles and battles.

> *Rejoice in the Lord always. I will say it again:*
> *Rejoice! Let your gentleness be evident to all.*
> *The Lord is near* (Phil. 4:4,5, *NIV*).

The first part of Paul's program is to rejoice in the Lord. It's not exactly a new theme with the apostle or even with this letter (see Phil. 3:1). But Paul doesn't mind repeating himself about something as important as rejoicing in the Lord.

Notice that he says to rejoice in the Lord *always*. Did your best friend move away? Rejoice in the Lord! Did you lose your job and therefore your source of spending money for Cokes and clothes? Rejoice in the Lord! Did your school just lose its umpteenth football game? Rejoice in the Lord!

"Now, wait a minute!" someone says. "Why should I rejoice when all this misery is happening?"

Well, we didn't say to rejoice in the misery. We said to rejoice in the *Lord*! And He is worth rejoicing about any time, anywhere, no matter what is happening. The Lord is "worthy to be praised" (Ps. 18:3, *NASB*).

So just how do you go about rejoicing in the Lord? One way is to begin with His Word. Open it to a psalm of praise—perhaps Psalm 148, which calls upon the whole creation to praise its Maker. Read the psalm over several times. Really tune in to what it is saying. Then start praying it back to God in your own way. For example:

The psalm says: *Praise the Lord! Praise the Lord from the heavens; praise Him in the heights!* (v. 1, *NASB*).

You respond: "Lord, I do praise you! You are so great a creator, you made the heavens and the heights!"

The psalm says: *Praise Him, all His angels; praise Him, all His hosts!* (v. 2, *NASB*).

You respond: "Lord, I rejoice in the sun and the moon! Thank you for making the sun to give us light to see by. Thanks for the way it makes us warm, and the way it makes my skin feel when it shines on me. Thank you for the way sunlight gives life to plants that look good and make oxygen and give us food.

"Thank you for the moon, which gives light at night. Thank you for the stars at night. It's not so easy to see them from a city, Lord, but when I'm out in the country they're really beautiful, and they remind me of you."

Get the idea? You're taking the things the Bible says, and you're using them to prime the pump of your own praise.

Another way to rejoice in the Lord is to think through everything you know about the Lord Jesus Christ—how He left the glories of heaven to become a man, how He grew up as a little child in the home of Joseph and Mary, how He started His ministry, how He healed and helped and taught the people until He died on the cross and rose again, and how He is in heaven preparing a place for you. Go through the story in your mind, filling in every detail you can remember. That'll make you feel like rejoicing!

Another good way to rejoice is to sing songs and hymns of praise. There are many excellent songs and hymns—from the very old to the very new. It's good to learn as many as you can, so you can sing them wherever you are. Then when things aren't going too well, or even just when you have a few minutes to kill while waiting for someone, you can sing a song or two and lift your heart to the Lord.

Don't Worry!

The next step to peace of mind, after rejoicing in the Lord, is to learn not to worry.

> *Do not be anxious about anything, but in everything, by prayer and petition, with thanksgiving, present your requests to God. And the peace of God, which transcends all understanding, will guard your hearts and your minds in Christ Jesus* (Phil. 4:6,7, NIV).

This is a familiar portion of Scripture. Is it so familiar we forget what it really means? Let's take a fresh look at it.

Don't be anxious—don't worry, Paul says. And we know that Paul is not some pie-in-the-sky preacher who never encountered a good reason to be anxious. This is the apostle, remember, who endured all kinds of hardships, beatings, stonings, imprisonments, shipwrecks, hunger, and other problems, for the sake of the gospel of Jesus Christ. The man who could sing hymns of praise to God in a Philippian jail, with his feet in stocks and his back a mass of bloody wounds (see Acts 16:22-25) is the man who can say, "Don't worry!" And those Philippian Christians weren't likely to forget it.

Still, it's not enough just to say "Don't worry," and Paul doesn't stop there. He tells us what to do about the things that we would worry about. Tell God about them!

If God is who and what He says He is, then His trusting child never needs to worry about anything. "Thou wilt keep him in perfect peace, whose mind is stayed on thee: because he trusteth in thee" (Isa. 26:3, *KJV*). God has promised peace of mind—but we have to give our worries to Him and trust Him and *keep our mind on Him*. Some of the things we talked about regarding rejoicing in the Lord will help here. When you're tempted to keep your mind on your worries, turn it to God instead by rejoicing in Him or singing songs of praise.

And don't forget to be thankful to God when you give Him your troubles. You don't know just how He will work them out, but you know He will do what is best for you.

"And we know that in all things God works for the good of those who love him, who have been called according to his purpose. For those God foreknew he also predestined to be conformed to the likeness of his Son, that he might be the firstborn among many brothers" (Rom. 8:28,29, *NIV*). God can take any circumstance, any hardship, and in that circumstance work for your good. And what is your good? To be conformed to the likeness of the Son! Sometimes the

Master Carpenter has to allow the sandpaper to dig deep; but the ultimate product is the more beautiful for it.

When you do what God says—giving your problems to Him, trusting Him, keeping your mind on Him, being thankful—then His peace will keep you safe. That peace, which is far beyond our ability to analyze and understand, will build a secure defense around both your heart and your mind—your emotions and your intellectual processes. Both need God's peace; both will receive it. Knowing God's peace is the best form of happiness there is.

PUT IT TO WORK

1. Do you have a concordance? If not, borrow one from a friend or from the church library. A concordance is a tool that helps you look up Bible words. An unabridged concordance lists every instance of every word in the Bible (usually based on the *King James Version*); an abridged concordance lists the instances and the words considered most important by the person who developed the concordance. Many Bibles have an abridged concordance in the back.

Now that you've found one, look up the word "rejoice"; then start looking up the Bible verses listed under "rejoice" in the concordance. Write down the ones that appeal to you the most with relation to rejoicing in the Lord and note what you learn from them. Do the same for "praise" and "thanks" or "thankful" or "thanksgiving."

Write out the verses you like best on cards or

135

notebook paper—something you can carry around in your purse or pocket. Next time you are tempted to worry or to get in a hassle about something, pull out your verses and spend some time rejoicing, praising the Lord, and thanking Him.

2. If you have trouble finding peace of mind, use the concordance to look up verses containing the word "peace." Write out the ones that mean the most to you and carry them with the others.

3. Even better than verses in your pocket are verses in your heart—so memorize some of them! Pick one or two to start with and work on them until you've got them down pat. Then do another, and another, until you have a whole arsenal of verses that you can use to shoot down every worry, frustration, anger or hassle that tries to get to you.

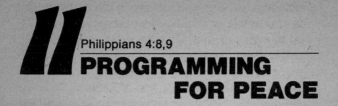

11
Philippians 4:8,9
PROGRAMMING FOR PEACE

Want to make a lasting impression?

Try this on your friends the next time you get together to rap: mention your psycho-cybernetic servo-mechanism.

Your *what*?

Well, that's as good a name as any. It's "psycho" because it's in your mind, "cybernetic" because it ties in with control and communication, "servo" because it's a relay device for monitoring your experiences and "mechanism" because it produces action and effect. In fact, you'd be a vegetable without it. That's why everybody's got one—though some are better trained than others.

On second thought, strike out the word "trained" and substitute the word "programmed." That makes it sound as if we carry a computer around in our heads, and that happens to be the truth.

That psycho-cybernetic thing is something inside your skull that records information, keeps it on file until it's needed and then calls it out for action.

You can verify the fact that you have a servo-mechanism by analyzing what happens when you walk. Go ahead. Get up and walk across the room and back. Who—or what—controls all those complex muscle groups that propel you forward so gracefully?

Stop me if I'm wrong, but I presume you don't find yourself saying, "I will now send a signal down to the biceps femoris behind my right thigh instructing these muscles to bend my knee and lift my right foot and leg. Now I'll tell my adductor longus and my rectus femoris to move the leg forward. Then, at precisely the right moment, I'll signal the extensor muscles in my right ankle to lift my foot slightly so that my heel touches the ground first. Meanwhile, I must tense a combination of muscles in my left leg sufficiently to propel my body forward but not enough to make me leap across the room."

Go at it that way and you'll make it to the breakfast table by lunchtime!

There's no need for all those detailed instructions. You've got built-in equipment to handle the whole process. It's the same when you swim, throw a baseball, play the piano or swallow your food. The computer takes care of the details.

Readout Depends on Input

But no matter how complicated the task of our cybernetic system, one thing remains true: the computer can base its readout only on the materials programmed in.

You won't find yourself reciting Shakespeare if you've never heard it before. You couldn't take up tennis on Monday and challenge Jimmy Connors at Forest Hills on Friday. He's been programming his computer since he was six years old. You'll never bang out a Chopin concerto the first time you face a piano keyboard. The cybernetic system gives out what it takes in. That's why we spend long hours learning and practicing. We're programming ourselves.

And that's the important fact that makes us different from a computer. We're responsible for the programming—at least, for a large percentage of it. Machines don't have a will, a conscience and a God-given sense of responsibility. They accept whatever's programmed in, and cough up their readouts accordingly.

Humans are able to control the input. We can make decisions about morals and values. We can pass judgment on the readout and say, "Here's proof of a memory bank that needs cleaning up. I've got a re-programming job to do." Only a change of input can remedy a problem that shows up in the output.

Since sex is said to be one of the most powerful forces in life, let's take that for an example. With some people, sex dominates huge chunks of their thought life. The reason is simple . They devote a lot of time to sensual input. Their memory banks are clogged with centerfold pictures, X-rated movies, "adult" magazines and little capers in the back seat of an automobile. What they think is what they are.

Or take hatred. Psychologists agree it's ridiculous for an intelligent human to let hatred for another person drain his spiritual and emotional resources, but millions of people do just that. Is someone often in your thoughts because he disgusts you so completely? Does a mental picture of his face haunt you day and night? If so, then the reason probably is that you *enjoy* hating him, and you feed that hatred more than you care to admit.

And what about covetousness? We're happy enough with what we have until we see someone with more—or with better. Then thoughts of what we don't have—what we'd *like* to have—fill our minds. Covetousness basically is being dissatisfied with what God sees fit to allow us, and a lot of people work hard at developing that dissatisfaction.

Yet we've agreed that people aren't really computers, and, unlike computers, don't have to settle for the cybernetic status quo.

We can reject the readout on grounds that it doesn't measure up to our ideals or suit our purpose. We can make changes in the material fed into the memory bank. When we take over decision-making responsibilities firmly enough and often enough we make the computer back off and accept its proper place, as our servant and not our master.

But the more we yield to the servo-mechanism and turn our backs on moral responsibility, the more strength the computer seems to gather, and the weaker we become. We become less able to control the output. The programming serves up data that moves us in a direction we'd really rather not move, and we find ourselves growing less able to fight back.

How many times have you said to yourself, "I know I shouldn't do things like that because the results are usually disastrous, but I can't seem to help myself"?

The fact is, we need to take control of the computer instead of letting the computer take control of us.

Control the Computer

Here's the way Paul puts it in two power-packed verses about that psycho-cybernetic servo-mechanism:

> *Finally, brothers, whatever is true, whatever is noble, whatever is right, whatever is pure, whatever is lovely, whatever is admirable—if anything is excellent or praiseworthy—think about such things. Whatever you have learned or received or heard from me, or seen in me—put it into practice. And the God of peace will be with you* (Phil. 4:8,9, *NIV*).

Paul never heard of computers, but he knew a lot about the right way to program the human brain. What you put in is what you get out. The way to have a happy life is to provide good input so you'll get good thoughts coming out. And he suggests several categories of good input for us to focus on. Let's take a look.

Think about whatever is true. That's basic. You can avoid a lot of resentment and grief by asking the simple question, "Is this *true*?" A lot of statements turn out to be figments or exaggerations of the imagination. Misunderstanding and misinterpretation often result in misinformation—and misinformation can work mischief in our relationships with other people.

At an even higher level, consider that God is the ultimate source of truth. When you have time for thinking whatever you choose to think, focus on God and His truth. Think about God's character—loving, kind, merciful, just. Think about what He has done for you through Jesus Christ, who is "the truth" (John 14:6). Program your computer with good thoughts like these until they crowd out the false values and phony attitudes of the world you live in.

Think about whatever is noble. That word "noble" may not be a top item in our twentieth century vocabulary, but it's worth looking at. It comes from a Greek word rarely used in the New Testament, and it has to do with being honorable or honest.

On one level, thinking of what is noble will help us maintain our self-respect. We keep from doing things or programming our computer with thoughts that will tear down our own character.

"I realized I couldn't respect someone who does things like that," Jeff explained to his pastor when he pulled out of a group of high school swingers, "so I guess I can't go on doing it and still have respect for myself." The teenagers had what they called a "sex circus" going—with a lot of pill popping and grass smoking to give it bigger kicks. Jeff is no longer part of the scene. Jeff was learning something about what it is to be noble in a biblical sense.

On another level, the most noble Being in the universe is our God, and the most honorable actions are His. If you really want to fill your mind with worthwhile stuff, read about, talk about, and think about the life Jesus Christ lived on this earth. Saturate yourself in His goodness, His other-centered life-style,

His down-to-earth naturalness and His total depenence upon the Father. That's the sort of program that will make your computer hum a happy tune!

Think about whatever is right. This category has to do with fairness and justice. It means we should work the question "Is it fair?" into our judgments about other people. If a thought about another person isn't fair or just, we need to keep it off the memory bank. An unfair thought is nothing but bad news when it gets into our psycho-cybernetic servo-mechanism.

When you see two of your friends talking and laughing together, do you jump to the conclusion that they're gossiping about you? *Unfair!* You can't possibly know what they're saying, so why jump to an unjust conclusion?

When your parents clamp down on your freedom to be out at night, do you assume that they're doing it out of meanness and a desire to keep you from having fun? *Unfair!* Maybe they're concerned because your health hasn't been tops lately and they want you to get more rest. Or maybe there has been a lot of assaults in your neighborhood lately and they want you to be safe. Be fair before you judge them.

Remember, too, that our Lord is the ultimate source of all that is right and fair and just. He will treat you fairly even if others don't. He can help you to see the fair way of looking at other people and their actions. And if you're really getting a raw deal somewhere, you can trust Him to work it out in the long run. "Do not take revenge, my friends, but leave room for God's wrath, for it is written: 'It is mine to avenge, I will repay,' says the Lord" (Rom. 12:19, *NIV*).

Think about whatever is pure. Don't fill up your computer with trashy input. You don't need to look at centerfold pictures. You don't have to join the others in their dirty stories in the locker room. Granted, it's hard to escape the billboards and the newspaper ads and all the other sources of not-so-pure input. But you don't have to dwell on them either.

Remember that impurity is not limited to sexual matters. Anything that tears down the things God advocates is impure—including disregard for human rights and taking human life lightly.

"Sincere" is another translation of the Greek word for "pure." If you're pure, or sincere, you won't give a glowing Christian testimony in the youth group on Sunday night, and then tear a friend's reputation to shreds at school on Monday morning. You won't fawn over a teacher in the hope of improving a grade damaged by your own lack of effort. You won't try to make yourself look good to the coach by practicing sly little maneuvers that put a teammate in a bad light.

And when you want something pure and sincere to think about, look to the Lord. Jesus Christ never flattered the powerful to win their favor. He told them the truth about themselves. Nor did He pull His punches when a close friend was making a terrible mistake: He spoke out forcefully to protect him from his error (see Matt. 16:21-23). He paid sincere compliments when they were appropriate (see John 1:47; Matt. 8:10). People loved Him because He was honest about Himself, about God, and about people.

Think about whatever is lovely. This means to con-

144

centrate on things that promote brotherly love. It's so easy to do the opposite—to gossip, to spread rumors, to nit-pick until you pick a fight. Paul says, "No, let's not look at our differences; let's look at the things that help us love one another."

Is somebody running down a friend? Bring up some of the friend's good qualities. Is someone picking a fight over a minor point of doctrine? Turn the conversation to things you can agree about—such as the wonderful love of Jesus Christ. Can't agree on how to get a job done? Suggest a break for prayer in which each person concentrates on the *reason* for getting the job done (to share Christ, to build believers up, to honor the Lord) and on seeking the Lord's way of getting it done.

In the quiet moments, when it's your own thoughts that are bugging you, focus on Jesus and His great love. Remember how He told His disciples to love one another as He loved them (see John 15:12,17). Ask for His love to fill you and overflow to others. Then you will be "lovely!"

Think about whatever is admirable. Here's a concept to go hand in hand with "lovely!" Concentrate on the admirable things in other people. They'll love you for it. And it will help them live up to their best potential. You don't have to gush about it, but it will encourage a friend if you can say, "You know, I appreciate the way you keep your cool in class when the others are picking on you for your Christian stand. You don't back down in your convictions about the Lord, but you don't lose your temper either." Or, "I like the way you encourage new believers so patiently. Sometimes the questions they ask make me want to laugh or shout at them, but you just calmly tell them what the Scripture says without putting them down at all." Or, "It really encourages me to keep going in the Lord when I see the way you're trusting Him in the middle of your problems. He's using you as an example to me. "

While you're looking for admirable traits in others, don't leave yourself out! So many of us have a habit of putting ourselves down and acting as though we were less than worthless. While it's true that we are incapable of pleasing God sufficiently to win our own salvation, it's also true that He loves us and considered us worth the sacrifice of His Son's life on the cross. Love what God loves—including yourself! And don't dishonor Him by denying the good qualities that He has put into your character and that He wants to develop further.

When you need a standard of comparison, take a look at the One who has every admirable trait in the universe—the One who made the universe and made admirable traits! Think of the Father's love and patience, His tenderness, His justice and righteousness. Look at the Son's obedience and self-giving love. Think of the Spirit's patient, self-effacing role as Teacher and Guide and Comforter. All eternity won't be long enough to call the roll of God's great attributes—to tell how admirable He is.

Think about whatever is excellent. How much of your time is spent in thinking and talking about the excellent things of life? This doesn't mean gourmet foods or luxurious clothes. It means the things that are excellent from God's point of view—love, mercy, justice, righteousness—that sort of thing. Our society doesn't exactly promote these concepts, so you have to swim against the tide if you want to develop God's idea of excellence in your life. But God will give you power to do it.

And He gives you His example, too. What could be a more excellent topic for thought or conversation than the Lord Himself?

Think about whatever is praiseworthy. The meanings of the words Paul uses have a tendency to overlap. But the apostle who is not afraid of repetition is also not afraid of overlapping meanings. He wants to get his idea across: Keep your thoughts on the things that are good!

Again we see that Paul isn't afraid to give himself as an example: "whatever you have learned or received or heard from me, or seen in me—put it into practice" (Phil. 4:9, *NIV*). "Do what I taught you," he says, "and do what you see me doing." Program your psycho-cybernetic servo-mechanism with the right kind of thoughts, and you'll know God's peace, for the God of peace will be with you.

Quite a formula for a happy life!

PUT IT TO WORK

1. Memorize Philippians 4:8,9 and try to find opportunities to use these standards in day-to-day experiences.
2. In what way can memorizing Bible verses be considered "programming" your psycho-cybernetic servo-mechanism?
3. Take a few quiet moments to yourself and think about the person you find the most difficult to put

up with. Actually close your eyes and try to conjure up a mental picture of that person's face. Can you be honest enough to label what you feel? Are bad vibrations starting already?

Now talk with God about your feelings. Try to imagine Christ reaching out in love to that person. Ask God to show you one thing about that person to be thankful for or something that is praiseworthy. Think on *that*.

Would it help if you set aside a few minutes every day to try to see that person in a better light? That's the kind of "programming" that fulfills Paul's requirements in the verses this chapter is based on.

12 KEYS TO CONTENTMENT AND PLENTY

Philippians 4:10-23

Someone, somewhere, sometime must have said it before, so I won't claim it as my own. It's a truth everyone has to wrestle with sooner or later: "Until you're able to be happy in *every* situation, you can't really be happy in *any* situation."

The trick is to get the right inflection on the key words. It might pay you to repeat that bit of wisdom out loud. Shut the door if you're afraid someone will think you've lost your mind. Then say it a few times to the mirror on the wall. Check it out for the best way to emphasize the words "every" and "any." It shouldn't take long before the truth comes through loud and clear.

Life is full of ups and downs—financially, physically, emotionally and every other way you can think of. The fact that you're on top of the heap today is no guarantee you'll be up there tomorrow. Your steady decides to go out with someone else. You blow a big exam and have to settle for a "D" in English. Someone you love and need moves away—or dies— or someone you're proud of falls off his pedestal.

A lot of our frustrations come because it's hard to be happy when the situation calls for dollar bills and the resources cough up only nickles and dimes.

Paul shares a great personal secret in the closing verses of Philippians. "I have learned to be content whatever the circumstances" (4:11, *NIV*). That's the shortest and best way he can find to sum it up. It may not sound like something all that revolutionary the first time you run it past, but the idea grows on you. If we can find the way to be happy in *every* situation, we'll soon discover we're actually happy in *any* situation—or vice versa. And that's achieving one of the most important goals in life.

In sharing that secret with the Christians at Philippi, the apostle apparently decides a good way to get his point across is to steer the conversation in the direction of money. As almost everyone knows, that can prove an effective way to get on people's nerves.

People are sensitive about money—especially if they suspect you aim to get your fingers in their pile. That's why now and then you hear little gems of wisdom like, "I'm just not interested in going to church, because all those preachers ever talk about is money!"

Some well-meaning ministers do get carried away with the financial needs of their church program, but that's no excuse for turning them off. People who preach sermons can goof like everyone else, and putting too much emphasis on the long green is an easy mistake to make. For some people it's a relative problem anyway. Nancy was a high school senior when she got ticked off at her pastor because he "begged for money" in two sermons in a row. She felt better about it, though, when she learned that people responded so generously the church was able to provide a $500 scholarship to help her enroll in a Christian college.

There's nothing sinful about silver coins and dollar bills. Even needing money and being concerned about it is nothing to be ashamed of. It's the *love* of money that's "the root of all evil" (1 Tim. 6:10, *KJV*). But respecting it and handling it with care is a far cry from a financial love affair.

In all Paul's contacts with Christians, no believers were more generous and dependable than his friends at Philippi. They had no sensitivity about "money talk." That's reflected in the fact that they sent Epaphroditus all the way to Rome with financial help for their missionary ambassador and beloved friend (see Phil. 2:25).

Gratitude and Contentment

You expect a man like Paul to be thankful for the kindness other people show him—and he is. In a sense, gratitude is the theme of the verses that follow —gratitude plus a contentment that can't be bought with money.

> *I rejoice greatly in the Lord that at last you have renewed your concern for me. Indeed, you have been concerned, but you had no*

opportunity to show it. I am not saying this because I am in need, for I have learned to be content whatever the circumstances. I know what it is to be in need, and I know what it is to have plenty. I have learned the secret of being content in any and every situation, whether well-fed or hungry, whether living in plenty or in want. I can do everything through him who gives me strength (Phil. 4:10-13, *NIV*).

Paul rejoices greatly—he's really glad—because the Philippian Christians have shown their concern for him in a practical way. They sent him a gift of money. As he thanks them, he takes the opportunity to share something he has learned in his years of serving the Lord.

"I have learned to be content." Paul doesn't say he got instant contentment the moment he received Christ. But through the years, as he grew in the Lord and went through many hardships and tough experiences, he *learned* to be content in any circumstance.

Probably some of the ideas in the previous verses had a lot to do with Paul's being able to be content. Remember, he's the one who sang songs of praise to the Lord in the jail in Philippi. He disciplined himself to rejoice in the Lord, to give his anxieties and worries to God, and to program his mind with positive thoughts. All of that certainly must have helped him to learn contentment.

Notice that Paul can be content "in want" *and* "in plenty." Some Christians seem to be happy only when they're "in plenty." If dad won't cough up the bucks for a car, Joe thinks he's terribly deprived. If mom suggests that Sue could work to earn the money for the extra clothes she wants, Sue thinks the world is coming to an end. American teens, perhaps more than any others, are used to "plenty." They find it hard to see how a person could be content and happy without all the goodies they enjoy.

There's another side to the coin—one that may not be such a problem to you. But it's worth a warning anyway. Some people get so ascetic that they're only content "in want." They aren't happy if they have "plenty." They feel guilty over having some nice clothes or a reliable car or a comfortable home. Maybe they're worried that God will make them "pay" later for what they're enjoying now. Maybe they're really down on themselves and feel they don't "deserve" the good things they have. Maybe they just don't understand that God doesn't mind His people enjoying some of the good things of life if they do it in the right spirit of loving Him and thanking Him for what they have.

The apostle Paul had no trouble. He could be content "in plenty" as well as "in want." Paul reveals the secret of his contentment in this statement: "I can do everything through him who gives me strength" (v. 13). It's God who helps Paul learn and practice contentment. It's God who gives him the power to rejoice in the Lord, to pray instead of worry, to fill his mind with good instead of trash.

Note that this verse does not mean that you can do *anything*. Some people take it that way. But you have to take Scripture in context. Paul is talking about dealing with the circumstances that life dishes out—or rather, that God *permits* in your life. If God puts you into a wealthy family, He will give you the strength to live as a Christian in the midst of plenty. If He puts you into a poverty situation, He will empower you to live for Him in the midst of want. If He lets you be persecuted for your faith in Him, He will show you how to handle it and give you strength to endure it. Even if He allows failure in your life, He will be with you through it, teaching you and strengthening you through the experience. You can do everything *God wants you to do*!

Christians Who Share

After telling of his contentment, Paul returns to the gift the Philippians had sent. He lets them know that he appreciates all they have done over the years, as well as their recent gift.

Yet it was good of you to share in my troubles. Moreover, as you Philippians know, in the early days of your acquaintance with the gospel, when I set out from Macedonia, not one church shared with me in the matter of giving and receiving, except you only; for even when I was in Thessalonica, you sent me aid again and again when I was in need. Not that I am looking for a gift, but I am looking for what may be credited to your account. I have received full payment and even more; I am amply supplied, now that I have received from Epaphroditus the gifts you sent. They are a fragrant offering, an acceptable sacrifice, pleasing to God. And my God will meet all your needs according to his glorious riches in Christ Jesus.

154

To our God and Father be glory for ever and ever. Amen (Phil. 4:14-20, *NIV*).

Sometimes we idealize the New Testament church, thinking that those early Christians were just about perfect and didn't have any of the problems we face today. A careful reading of the New Testament will quickly dispel that idea! Here Paul reveals a very modern sounding problem: the difficulty of getting some Christians to give money for missions.

The church in Philippi was the only one that had contributed to the support of Paul's missionary journey at one time. Paul expresses his thanks to the Philippians for their support.

Then he says something interesting: "Not that I am looking for a gift, but I am looking for what may be credited to your account" (v. 17). Paul has already explained his secret of contentment. He has proved in his own experience that he can take anything that comes along, either "want" or "plenty." He appreciates the gift, but almost more for the Philippians' sake than for his own. He assures them that it will be credited to their account. God notices what His people do, and He gives them credit for their good deeds. This is part of His love and His justice.

The Lord Jesus spoke of this also: "Do not store up for yourselves treasures on earth, where moth and rust destroy, and where thieves break in and steal. But store up for yourselves treasures in heaven, where moth and rust do not destroy, and where thieves do not break in and steal. For where your treasure is, there your heart will be also" (Matt. 6:19-21, *NIV*).

The things you do to serve the Lord, the money

you give, the fruits of Christian character that you develop—all these go into your account in heaven. Other people may not notice, but God does. The Lord who knows the number of hairs on your head (see Matt. 10:30) won't slip up and forget any of the things that are to be credited to your account.

Have you spent time counseling a new Christian instead of going to the beach? God knows about it. Do you spend time each week at a retirement home cheering up the elderly residents and running errands for them? The Lord has taken note of it. Have you given your birthday money to help buy food for the local rescue mission? God has credited it to your account. Have you made a determined effort, with God's help, to put profanity and vulgarity out of your vocabulary? God has added that effort to your treasure in heaven.

It can be very encouraging to remember that your treasure in heaven is growing according to what you do here on earth. You don't have to be so concerned about *people* noticing what you do when you know that *God* notices and appreciates your gifts of service. As Paul says in Philippians 4, "They are a fragrant offering, an acceptable sacrifice, pleasing to God" (v. 18).

At the same time, you have to watch your motivation a bit. Your heavenly treasure grows when you do things out of love for the Lord and for your fellow human beings. It might not grow at all if your primary thought is getting credit for your good deeds.

You need a balance in your thinking. After all, the Lord Jesus Himself spoke about your treasure in heaven, and the Holy Spirit inspired Paul to write about crediting gifts to your account. God obviously wants us to know about and be encouraged by these facts. But it's not a good idea to make that heavenly treasure your main motivation for what you do.

God and Your Finances

After assuring the Philippians that God has credited their gift to their account, Paul gets even more practical. God doesn't limit His caring to a heavenly bank account. He cares about us and helps us right here, right now. "My God will meet all your needs according to his glorious riches in Christ Jesus" (v. 19).

Once again, we need to be careful to understand this verse in its context. The Philippians, who had little money to begin with, gave a sacrificial gift to the Lord's work. In return, Paul says, God will meet their needs. You can't take this verse as a promise that God will meet your needs even when you aren't living for Him, or that He will meet your needs when you've got enough money to meet your own needs. But when you give to God out of your lack like the widow with her small coins (see Luke 21:1-4), then God will meet your needs.

This is another way of saying what Jesus said about giving: "Give, and it will be given to you. A good measure, pressed down, shaken together and running over, will be poured into your lap. For with the measure you use, it will be measured to you" (Luke 6:38, *NIV*). Get hold of that image. If you give to God, God will give back to you so much that it's like filling up a bushel basket: You shake it to settle the contents, you push it down, and then it still runs over. If you're generous with God, He'll be super-generous with you. But if you're selfish and stingy, you don't give God much to work with, and He won't be able to be super-generous with you. If you use a teaspoon for giving to God, He'll use a teaspoon with you. If you use a bushel basket in proportion to what *you* have, God will use a bushel basket in proportion to what *He* has. (And He has a whole lot more than you do!)

Really get hold of this fact: If you give to God, He will take care of your needs. Really grasp that, and you will be freed from your fears about money. You, your youth group, your Sunday School, your whole congregation, can be released from money worries!

Take a look at some sample worries about money:

"Dave's idea would be a great shot in the arm for our young people's program, but where'd we ever get the money to do it?"

"One of those modern translations sure would help me understand the Bible, but my baby-sitting money just won't stretch that far."

"That trip to Smoky Ridge Camp would be just right to reach those new kids with the gospel, but the deacons say the church budget can't afford it."

How about restating those propositions, this time with a firmer grip on the idea of God's involvement in our financial affairs? How about a second look at these golden opportunities, this time with a genuine confidence in the power of God to support His own program here on earth?

"Dave has a great idea there, and if we'll all put our faith to work, I'm sure we can find a way to get the money."

"I believe the Lord wants me to understand and apply His Word better, so if I pray about it and try as hard as I can I'm sure He'll help me buy a modern translation to use in my Bible study."

"Let's ask the deacons to meet with us so we can explain the evangelistic strategy we plan to use at Smoky Ridge Camp. Together, we probably can change a few priorities and get that important activity on the budget."

That's the kind of language Christians ought to speak. It's the language of optimism and assurance.

God's personal involvement in our money matters makes us responsible to be generous with others. It frees us from fear and anxiety about finances. God does know how it is—or isn't—with us, and He does care. He is willing and able to supply what we need.

Not what we *want* always, but what we truly need. As long as we shoulder our own responsibility and trust Him for the impossibilities, He'll never let us down.

Final Greetings

And now it's time for Paul to wrap it all up and hand his happy letter over to Epaphroditus to be delivered to the church at Philippi. He does it with a parting note that says again, "It's really great to be a believer in Jesus Christ!"

Greet all the saints in Christ Jesus. The brothers who are with me send greetings. All the saints send you greetings, especially those who belong to Caesar's household.
The grace of the Lord Jesus Christ be with your spirit (Phil. 4:21-23, *NIV*).

Philippians ends as it began, on a happy note. It tells us that deep-down satisfaction is never the result of conditions alone. It doesn't stand or fall on what people do to us or for us. It flows from inside. It comes only from God.

Even in decidedly unhappy situations, believers in Jesus Christ have in their possession the raw materials from which true happiness is made.

PUT IT TO WORK

1. Try to write out in three or four sentences an accurate description of the situation you're in right now that causes you the most concern. Does it involve school, finances, personality conflict, family problems? Probably you've never put it into words before. We aren't able to solve problems until we get them out in the open and identified. That's one good reason for writing out this description.

2. How would that problem be affected if you changed your attitude from negative to positive? Can you see a possible purpose God might have in allowing you to experience this difficulty? If so, try writing out this sentence: "I believe God's purpose for me in this problem is . . ." and complete the sentence in your own words.

3. Get acquainted with Philippians 4:19 and Luke 6:38. Do you have money problems? Could it be that you haven't been giving enough to God? Ask God to help you understand what He wants you to give—then trust Him to meet your needs!